The Grand Piano

The Grand Piano
PART 3

An Experiment in Collective Autobiography
San Francisco, 1975–1980

Steve Benson   Tom Mandel

Carla Harryman   Rae Armantrout

Lyn Hejinian   Bob Perelman

Barrett Watten   Ted Pearson

Kit Robinson   Ron Silliman

Detroit ■ 2007

Design by Barrett Watten (after Varvara Stepanova).

Mode A is an imprint of This Press, published by Barrett Watten, 6885 Cathedral Drive, Bloomfield Township, MI 48301 or Department of English, Wayne State University, 5057 Woodward Avenue, 9th Floor, Detroit, MI 48202.

http: // www.english.wayne.edu / fac_pages / ewatten

The Grand Piano began serial publication in November 2006. It is planned to appear at three-month intervals and will number ten volumes when complete. Subscription to the series is available for $90 from Lyn Hejinian, 2639 Russell Street, Berkeley, CA 94705.

Distributed by Small Press Distribution, Inc., 1341 Seventh Street, Berkeley, CA 94710-1409.

ISBN 978-0-9790198-2-1 / 128 pp., $12.95 paper

I am I because my little dog knows me, even if the
little dog is a big one, and yet the little dog know-
ing me does not really make me be I no not real-
ly because after all being I I am I has really noth-
ing to do with the little dog knowing me, he is
my audience, but an audience never does prove
to you that you are you.

—Gertrude Stein,
THE GEOGRAPHICAL HISTORY OF AMERICA

NEARLY THIRTY YEARS AGO, in the fall of 1976, Carla and I moved to San Francisco. Soon we separated, amicably, definitely, remaining fast friends. In the winter, in the apartment on Hampshire Street in the Mission District that I still shared with her brother after she left, I kept an untitled journal that indicates I was preoccupied by thoughts about being with women and being with men and the ways one may as a man be with women and what I wanted in intimacy and my uncertainty about it all.

> *So many thoughts going through my head lately I feel stupid – I don't know what to do w/ them.*

Today I am sitting in a rented apartment in Maine overcoming hernia surgery, more slowly than expected. I can't stand up straight and pain accumulates quickly when I walk. As back then, I don't know what to do or whether what I do is worthwhile, but now I cannot go about.

Plainly, decidedly, I was writing down how and trying to learn why I was feeling guilty, afraid, anxious, confused, inept or incapacitated in my relations with people I was attracted to or seeking some kind of dependency with. Maybe I was depressed, after the break-up, at a loss, anxious and frightened.

Once a week I saw a young psychotherapist at a public clinic, free because my income was so slight. After a while she complained of being bored with me. I expected her to cut me if I asked her for advice.

<u>Recurrent feeling</u>: I'm bad for women.

I seem to have felt preoccupied by others' dependence on me. I was aware this might be my delusion. I was aware of seeking to be supported, utterly, by another. And who is this *me*, this *I*, perpetually reacting to himself, others the reflection of his need —who or what?

> meanwhile dishwashing
> and yet not a sore throat
> the peasant <u>is</u> real
> that she might be taking smthg from me
> the way I am Shakespeare – king of his own
>   world's making, all responsive to him, made to
>   us by his own created world, king of the coop
> the peasant is present
> Shakespeare is past + timeless – he owes smthg
>   to the peasant
> writing as they will read for the author leads me
>   to fiction + evasion? the truth in that (not so
>   billiard ballish)
> creation of a 3rd self to mediate + resolve between

body/peasant + king/mind – the artwork or
dream puts it together – the artwork puts it
outside of me, where I can "face it" at once
to show my control, express myself? afraid to
realize I don't have to do it that way – the van-
ity in that work that I want to "get rid of," the
claim that "this isn't it"
what's "it" she asks again

title: life without raisins

visual track to the poetry reading
Carla telling me nightmare of being shot in the
    head
when I'm too tired
change title to "Untold Stories of Well-Known
    Words"
note to Adrian: illness, L.A., "friendliness?" –
bray cough howl bark

When I begin to think my life is all a lie
I can't write well
I can't think well

There are all sorts of comments, writings,
notes laid into this journal, the cover of which bears
the legend "CUADERNO GALGO" under grey and black
silhouettes of racing greyhounds. How brutally

grave the self-consciously analyzed relationships appear. Did I not know how to play? Just what choice was I avoiding, in favor of what worry? I struggled to shed an identity of sheer delight and surprise at my circumstances and activity. I suspected it as self-deceptive and naive, as if such ingenuousness were constraining me in an immature presumption—

the identity of a prodigy

But this meant writing off what I had most liked in myself. I couldn't really drop the heart of it.

What was I seeking in its place? Responsibility? The ability to respond, to integrate reaction and reflection in resolve, in action—I figured maybe it was that. Meanwhile, I hovered in gay bars, seeking to recognize the ideal in men I could rarely approach. It was dark in there, with garish color highlights and imaginary flickering halos. I was looking for the artist who would check me out. Is there anyone here who would like to be me? As if my goal were to discover someone to embody this role, about whom I could fantasize afterward.

■

I WAS ALSO LOOKING for truth, through desire. In effect, if we were not locked in perfect easeful bliss eternally,

I would just wrack myself on frustration's perplexing iron bed. I felt certain I deserved something more real, palpable—release—and that I must be holding out on myself—how? By my shyness, my mentality? Running in circles, I kept glimpsing myself from behind just before disappearing round the corner.

> I wanted him to kiss me on the lips and fold me in his embrace so I paused forever, told him I was very nervous, asked him if he wrote that poem about me, told him I was about too dizzy, finally that I was very affected by having a conversation about sex with him once before, and unsure of my feelings but compulsively concerned lest I had hurt him, i.e., done the wrong thing. He left later bewildered but reassuring me I hadn't done the <u>wrong</u> thing. (After pointing out that I still seemed to be having some problems about breaking up with Carla. His poem had been about his her. I never wrote poems re Carla until we broke up.

> girl: Say I notice you been spending a lotta time w/ Sammy lately hunh? other girl: yeah. girl: so you havin a good time hunh? other girl: yeah, he's nice to me. girl: you like him? other girl: yeah I like him.
> girl: ooohhhhhhhh . . . . ! other girl feels fate grab

hold of her through every follicle – her emo-
tion has been discovered.

for at least a couple of days, continual
pressure of anxiety.
Shock.
                sauna + a good artist
+ a good dinner   (Douglas Woolf)
(Carla) + theorizing together about depression:
accept the fact that I'm in it (rather than trying
to analyze its roots or formulize its resolution or
otherwise psych it out) – let go of it
that way (set no deadlines, plan no fears
of the future)

assignment: 2 nights a week in meeting places of
homosexual men, including 3 or more conversa-
tions with strangers

I have to think hard now whether to go to the bath-
room. To go there. I type over the dull pain in my ab-
domen where they cut and patched, the pressure in
my penis, swollen after surgery. No one here but me.
After I use the toilet, the wound stings more a while.
I skip ahead to another part of the journal that I
want to show you. The first paragraph is inscribed a
little wildly, as though I were waking from a dream,
writing in the dark or drunk:

a party. blah blah blab la bah ha be aurf so forth
till I act I like acting. Ganging up on a person – all
a projection. Go to the arts bkstore tomorrow,
ask David what he felt, tell him I don't know,
totally disoriented? Wha bull. night now no
glasses yet can focus w/ distractions, driving fine
once out of park. a fact, not a metaphor – <u>not</u> a
metaphor. ah. mahogany baloney. let's talk
about what I know about (ie, better than you) <u>or</u>
what you may now defend to me –

The indications abound. I whisk an eye across
the sty – the field. Forgetting last week almost
completely, remembering only what I have put
into words, as even then I felt I was distorting the
experience because my words would be repeat-
ed afterwards in my head, even if my lips begged
to differ with them.

■

Lecture topics: masturbation/gothic churches/
bookstore clerk/Coltrane/daubigny and corot/
wall decorations in my apartment/— use huge
newsprint pad to draw on in charcoal during
talks or to have drawings already prepared on
(to be shown irregardless of actual content but
covering same subjects). – drawings done in

advance + during/ — tapes (2 of them?) w/ soft musical backgrounds, street noises — / duration established by length of tape +/or assistant's timed turning of pages (1 hr, 1 ½ hrs, 45 min?) — / walking on sts/comparison of cities/andy warhol/ — have notes prepared on the file cards to fill in with talk/reviews of movies – have each member of the audience write name of a movie on a file card + pass them in for off the cuff reviews – every other topic will be a movie review/

lecture topic: making an aesthetic out of my parents in me.

3rd floor   552–3668 Bookstore
David Highsmith   863–3879

an autolecture. a group participatory lecture. I (a leader) go around whispering a topic +/or questions +/or attitudes in ears of various individuals (everyone in audience). They retell it or respond to it or say something else or say nothing out loud. The group hears me through its parts. "Telling what you know about." Telling what you know about what I say I know.

No "AUTOLECTURE" ever occurred in just this way, and although I have forgotten some of these ideas until transcribing them today, I can see they've informed all my talks and improvisational performances in the years since then. They open questions concerning the ability to respond, in various ways. I must have been anticipating my first presentation in the Talks series Bob was beginning at the railroad studio apartment he and Francie rented. Bob must have asked me to think about what I would talk about.

In the talk I soon put on, "Views of Communist China," I gave a tour of my current apartment, the décor of which had been moved into Bob and Francie's for the evening. The idea was modeled on the tours of the palace at Monaco and the White House that Grace Kelly and Jackie Kennedy had given on TV, which I had never seen. In the event, my presentation continually and increasingly broke down into give and take with the group assembled to hear it, as they made questions and commented on the environment, the situation, and one another's remarks, the form and content of our joint experience emerging through this netting of words. The ruptured tour of my apartment was bracketed by my two deadpan recitations from memory of speeches by contemporary Chinese peasants, which I had transcribed from a *New Yorker* article by Orville Schell. Joining this performance with the coalescing community of the incident *was* a revelation to me, which I reacted to immediately by preparing a precise transcription and packaging it between covers with photographs of the event by John Harryman (who later, under my direction, snapped my picture for my first book cover).

Typing had long been a species of realization to me, whether of absurdist fantastical daydreams channeled into stories at pubescence, letters to beloved friends that assured me when in doubt that my relationships were genuine, or poems that turned careless momentary wrinkles in my imagination into tentative gestalts. The poem appeared, at times, to portend me, yet it always pointed somewhere else, its insistence on difference as necessary as that of a Warhol detergent carton or the Beatles cover of an R&B song.

Around that time I had written a letter to my parents, coming out as a gay man. This was throwing my hat in the ring. I must have felt I had hesitated so long on their account. My internalized them, Midwesterners who had slipped the knot of family roots, pulling together a game show for the sake of Princeton society. I had always been the nice son, devious, against the grain, but proprietorial and pacifist. If I were gay, perhaps I would be whole, reckless, honest, joyous, fine. But I bet I told them soberly, with all diplomacy intact. I was dissatisfied with their responses in their two separately thoughtful and considerate letters,

> each sentence a pivot btwn 2 attitudes, neither re-
> flecting the feeling I want to know underneath it.

Later in the notebook, I wrote that they had both explained that my disclosure changed nothing in their feelings for me or our relationships. This left me feeling angry and humiliated, after having so long sheltered them from my urgent internal Q&A.

> in fact I'd been going though great efforts of self-
> repression for their sakes in order (I thought) not
> to burden them with it or lead them to devalue
> or worry over me (or themselves). They con-
> firmed that all that energy had been wasted —
> that either it didn't matter in terms of their love
> for me, or else that they weren't going to show it
> did (so—differences in degree or ease or warmth
> of feeling are not to be admitted into expression.
> so—all expression of feeling may be somewhat
> bogus)

Weren't *they* going to feel angry or humiliated, anxious or guilty? They were polite and discreet, leaving me on my own again. Out of respect, care, for themselves and for me.

The result seems to have been a terrific release of ease, however, an allowance of appreciation for myself, as is.

> <u>Why</u> should I worry whether I'm self-indulgent,
> uncontrolled, behaving or speaking in ways
> unacceptable to others?
> I judge <u>them</u> by their behavior – if I don't know/
> trust that I like them yet. e.g., his talk, its mass, its
> degree of clarity, its attn to my needs, its elocu-
> tion. And yet here is someone who is just what I
> want, I keep nothing to myself – and indeed,
> there is nothing I think wrong in him.

Throughout the journal, as so often in the poetry, the human referent is often left unclear. Today, even the names of the young men I wished to have a crush on are ciphers to me, no matter what I quote them saying, but in some passages like that above it's obscure whether I mean myself or another. Implicit was the choice to let the writing stand on its own, released from narrative, without denying that the story mattered too—but separately, differently.

The decision to insist unapologetically, if possible, on what might be construed as vanity and solipsism is a social practice, in this case—taking a risk of making a difference by being different, in my turning of it, from what I'd been tacitly asked to perform (the good soldier). To be willing, instead, to open myself to love, to judge in the affirmative. (As, it now seems, my parents had chosen to, even while they kept some of their feelings to themselves, being good soldiers.)

Now the journal of that winter gets more full of plans, comments, and trials of poetry writing and performances. These are tactics for showing up among my peers—my chosen people.

At the Actualist Convention in Berkeley on April 16, 1977, I improvised a twenty-minute performance as my mother and my father when they were children in their parents' homes, changing between a dress and a shirt and pants, silent before a flickering projector with someone else's hands carving abstractions out of its cast light. The next day Carla and I read in an Open Studio series, curated by Bob, including three collaborations we had written with four other friends—not Language poets, but friends. Four days after the "Views of Communist China" talk, I made a classroom appearance at San Francisco State University in connection with a performance that evening (at age twenty-seven, my sixth new presentation within seven months)—like other performances, presented in the context of a poetry reading, if not a lecture—and first projected through a suggestion in the notebook, an exact and accurate sketch:

> poetry reading: create elaborate mockup of livingroom/study. improvise preparations and rehearsals for a reading, inc. stream of conscious-

ness chatter, choosing poems, playing records … indulge emotions

lecture: mockup of entire apartment – in another space [or do it in my apartment] – tour of apartment, improvised. as though I/we were there (as many as I want to imagine) – what I wd <u>want</u> to show, tell + do.

Buy candles. I can sit in the room too full from dinner + all the conversation, turn out the lights and listen to "Black Diamond Bay" for half the song and it seems like 10 minutes and I don't even think about a thing about the song except how strong the tone is. I'm thinking of other things: notes for the reading at Brannan Street to introduce the trilogy that ends in "The Games," just as this is a note to prepare for my talk in Bob's series and a positive footnote to my reading at 3rd Floor Books. If I'd had candles I wouldn't have had to turn on the lights to write this. Now – to work!

Oedipus myth / being <u>in love</u> with her! Wanting a chair I can curl up + read in. "… any introversion in later life regresses back to infantile reminiscences .." writing as escape into subjectivity, cut off abruptly but neatly when organized directed thought betrays its attention. She peeps her

■

YOU ALWAYS SEEMED so mature and worldly, though, as if you already knew what you thought, thought better of it, and knew what to say, but would recklessly blurt out something it amused you to toss off instead, delightedly surprised to find yourself already present. I thought I'd get into trouble if I were you, fearlessly affectionate and cavalier—in a possibly noble way. Imagine slipping into one another's lives for a while—how perplexed and disappointed you would be! Or into one another's selves—would that have changed our lives?

 I WAS MUCH older than you when we met in 1976. The difference narrowed over time, and I suppose it may be increasing again. I would not—probably I could not—have written a journal with the

introspective concentration of yours. The questions had not gone away, but I had been listening to my answers for too many years.

Worldly—not a pose, although perhaps it felt that way at times, to others and even to me; nor was it my character exactly. An emotional trope, say.

I'd grown up early. I was married before I was twenty-one, a father of two at twenty-four, divorced at twenty-seven. In 1976 I turned thirty-four, my father's age when he died. I'd lived in Chicago, New York, and Paris before San Francisco; I'd had several careers—college professor, editor, research writer for UNESCO. But, at some point during the three years since my late night knock on David Degener's door at 492 Laguna Street I had decided stay off any path that might lead to another career, the last thing I wanted.

■

MY FIRST JOB in San Francisco didn't last long. In early 1974, I worked as a short order cook at Andy's, a coffee shop on Castro Street. The job paid next to nothing, but by then I was broke. I had the night shift, coming on at 11 P.M. and leaving at 7 in the morning. The gay bars closed at 2 A.M., and Andy's filled up with transvestites. Big hair, big bejeweled and nail-painted hands, big red lips, and big appetites

    TM

too. As with so many men in their twenties, and I had
been the same way, breakfast seemed just the thing in
the middle of the night. It made an odd juxtaposi-
tion, the large, oval plate holding three-egg omelet,
hash browns, bacon, toast or short stack, and the
glamorous creature in shining bouffant wig, dressed
for the Oscars, before whom I set down the plate.

I worked my shift alone. I prepped, cooked,
delivered food, cleaned tables, and washed and dried
dishes. Here was a concentration of desire. One
night, slicing tomatoes, I took a flap of skin and
flesh off my right thumb (I'm left-handed). I
wrapped a bandage around the cut, but I had to
work the dishwasher, and there was no way to keep
the wound dry. For the next few hours, every plate
I delivered had a spot of blood on its rim. I was fired
the following day.

■

THE STORY I JUST told echoes Steve's journal but par-
odies it as well. As in the journal, we see the author
struggling for effect in a context of sexual ambigui-
ty. My story is true, but the struggle portrayed is of
a lower order. I play Caliban, as against Steve's Duke
—whose tempestuous mind is in exile, *seeking* the
world but not *of* the world, not *worldly*. This has been
intentional, yet what is its intention?

What stunned me in Steve's journal was the way its insistent uncertainty led the writer to undertake such original and bold work, as if doubt's shadow could shine in bronze. This was the way Steve seemed to me at the time too. His reticence, like my worldliness, was a trope. Delicate, shifting, and sinuous. But I missed "Views of Communist China," I think I was out of town.

■

STEVE'S CHARACTERIZATION of me as worldly seemed apt the moment I read it, and now that I've acted out the aptitude, making it present rather than figuring upon it, I see that as with any syntactic figure, from juxtaposition to the most complex trope, this use of language both represents and also invokes the destiny of its object. You know me now, dear reader, as Steve knew me then.

In a notebook from that time, I wrote, "He wants to sleep beneath a single light that breaks up meditation. In view of a bird slamming against our window a faceless body kisses force goodbye." The first sentence recalls a bulb hanging from a wire in a sooty, seventh-floor walk-up in Paris, a *chambre de bonne*—maid's room—where I lived for a few months in early 1973; *nostalgie de la boue*. The room held a cold water sink and a worn mattress on the floor. A small dormer window looked out on Paris rooftops and the cold blue sky. At the end of a long evening, after I'd climbed to my little room, I was a puzzled and sometimes a happy man. Everything is temporary; it can be nice when it tells you so.

I wrote my mother with my new address and heard back from her that she and my father had lived in that building in 1939. To elude the Sureté, my father had slept many nights in one of the maids' rooms, perhaps the one where I now found myself.

At the time, I was studying with an extraordinary man, an elderly Chinese philosopher living out his late seventies in Paris after having lived his twenties there as well. A professor of French at Peking University at the time of the revolution, he'd been under house arrest for two decades, then had been released and managed to return to France.

When he was young, Chien wrote a book of poems in French, called *Ma mère*, to which Paul Valéry contributed an introduction. I told him about my mother's letter, and he responded immediately that I should leave Paris. "This place is old, filled with the past and death. The past makes me young, but it will make you old." A month or so later, I returned to the U.S.

I'll tell more of Chien's story another day.

In the second sentence, both the bird and the faceless body must evoke the writer's then-current state. I can tell you no more. Those sentences found their way into *Ready to Go*, a book of poems from the early 70s that Ithaca House published in 1981.

■

BY 1976, I WAS a CETA artist, working for San Francisco's Community Arts Program. I spent much of my time writing grant proposals for small arts groups. The gig lasted almost two years, the longest period in the last thirty that anyone has written me a paycheck. I moved to a flat on Waller Street that year, right around the corner from the Grand Piano. When I began going to the readings, and then curating the series with Ron, we started having post-reading parties at my place.

At parties, readings, and talks in those years, I was often annoyed by how tall everyone else in the room was. Alan and Kit had gone to Yale, and both were tall; Steve was a Yale graduate, and I thought Bob was too; they were both taller than I, and seemed to gain height from their schoolfellows as well. But, I learned last week, Bob had gone to Michigan, not Yale. At 6' 1", Barry was right up there with Alan, though he did have to look up to Kit. I remember Warren Sonbert and his partner Ray Larsen, also tall, talking in my kitchen with Alan and Kit. A conversation on another level, liter-

TM

ally. I was happy that some of my new friends—Lyn, Ron, Carla, Ted, and a few others—didn't loom over me. Rae often wore big platform shoes that made her seem tall. She wasn't though, when they came off.

A few weeks after Warren moved west, we were introduced by Phillip Lopate, who was visiting from New York. A week or so later, Warren and I went together to a matinee of Sam Fuller's *The Big Red One* somewhere out on the Avenues; we had a great conversation, and I invited him to a party at my place, where he met a few more of us. Warren and I became close friends. We admired each other's work, but perhaps it was, again, *worldliness* that sealed our friendship. I was married to Gaelyn Godwin then, before she became a Buddhist priest (but without losing her worldliness), and when Ray came along, the four of us started having dinner together about once a week and continued the practice for years.

Much later, in 1995, Beth and I left Warren's deathbed to attend my daughter Sarah's graduation from medical school. My mother had been a medical student in Vienna. After the *Anschluss* and emigration, she had been unable to resume her medical education. Today, she draped Sarah's shoulders with the cape that represented her degree. Lyn's daughter Anna graduated in the same class. Leaving the ceremony, Lyn and I ran into each other. The day was bright; we walked together a few steps on the white marble plaza. I don't remember our conversation except that Lyn used the word *splendid,* and I recalled then that it was a word she favored. A few days ago I read Bob's contribution to this volume and responded, "This is splendid." As I hit "send" and the e-mail disappeared, that graduation day rose whole and splendid in my mind.

After the ceremony, Beth and I returned to Warren's place on 21st Street. I had been reading to him from Shelley's "Adonais," urging him to move on. He died a few days later, in early June. The following January, my mother died.

> Leave it ragged
> That small a thought
> Fills a life.
> Sow ideas, reap ideas.
> Ash covers embers.
> What we know dies.
> A fire in the mind.
>
> Every stroke he makes
> Tunes the instrument.
>
> —"Mute Canto (I)," REALISM

■

STEVE, YOU ASKED ME once, "Why do you write?" I may have been offended by the question. I may have thought that, being asked, the question meant that the work did not justify its existence but required something additional, a "reason I write." I answered that writing was the only thing I found difficult, really difficult; that was my reason to write.

Nothing permanent, zero is real. Permanent feet polish cement to marble. Spirits have a measure of thought not to our measure wrought. Not sought as measure taught.

—"Mute Canto (II)," REALISM

Playing Memory
In Memoriam Philip Horvitz: 1960–2005

If I tell you one thing I remember, you will think I'm an idiot for remembering only one thing.

—Pelican, MEMORY PLAY

IN THE EARLY 1990s I wrote and staged a play called *Memory Play*. The first act was composed on a blue and silver electric typewriter on top of an old-fash-

ioned wooden schoolteacher's desk in a couple of sittings, but other than that I curiously remember little about writing it; whereas, the completion of the work I remember with greater intensity and detail, even as this activity took place at the same desk with the same typewriter. I am sure this has something to do with the degree of excitement I feel in working with other people. I hadn't been motivated to finish the play until I showed the first act to artist John Woodall while I was over at his studio looking at skeletal things he'd scavenged from the Florida Keys. He wanted to get right to work on *Memory Play*, as he was taken with its setting, "a little tent town out in the salt flats," and its *dramatis personae*: Fish, Reptile, Pelican, Child, Instruction, and Miltonic Humiliator.

But we agreed it needed another act. I completed the writing by sending John a scene a week by post, using the first act of the play as the map for the second. I convinced theater artist Philip Horvitz to direct it, then we set about arranging to stage it at The LAB, a public artspace founded in the late 1970s, which was then located on Clement Street. It had a great storefront gallery space that allowed us to construct the set facing outward toward the street, perfect for the exposed salt flat encampment and carnivalesque collectivity of its *mise en scène*. Part of the staging ultimately involved dragging a truckload of sand on sheets into the front of the gallery as John, a naturalist as well as an artist, understood the relationship between sand and salt.

In the storefront of The LAB, we performed memory but not in a conventional sense. We weren't remembering anything except the text. Rather than locating itself thematically in a problem of or about memory, the play plays memory as a kind of unpredictable instrument. As instigated by the musings and exchanges of the play's human/nonhuman community, memory appears as performative, mechanical, motivated, intersubjective, (de)territorial, communal, and necessary to language. The San Francisco cast, selected to mess up the orthodoxies of staged works, additionally reflected the diversity and communality of the play's engagement with versions, sampling, all kinds of attributes of memory.

Since the first draft of this entry the director of *Memory Play*, Philip Horvitz, has died. He was forty-four years old when his heart stopped beating while he was on a plane between New York and San Francisco, where he was headed to attend his brother Bill's wedding in Sonoma County. Because of heart trouble, the San Francisco engagement following the wedding would have been his first solo performance in many years.

To say the least, Philip was an intense actor. One of the most energetic performances I have ever seen was his solo show *Yes, I Can*, a version of the life of Sammy Davis, Jr., complete with appropriated memoir and familiar songs. There was a catch, however. The text and songs went around twice in an exact repetition. The work was no longer a version of the life but a conceptual displacement of performed desires that betray the possibility of transcendence. *Yes, I Can* did not exhaust itself so much as strip away every shred of sentimentality from Sammy Davis, Jr.'s life story. Philip's rendition was a not-uncontroversial act of devotion and critique. Not everyone in his audience easily accepted a white gay man playing the part of Sammy Davis, Jr., and Philip thought about the politics of this controversy nondismissively for the next twelve years.

The work was performed to sell-out crowds at Josie's Cabaret and Juice Joint on 16th Street, a lively gay club on the edge of the Castro: it had a longer than anticipated run. Barrett and I were in one of these crowds, which I would characterize as riveted crossed with back-talking. The hard-as-glass *détournement* of the work with its twice-told effects was a political and aesthetic intervention into the realm of grand American fantasies—notched way up to match the brilliant, devastated, and AIDS-politicized scene of San Francisco 1990s queer culture.

For me, one of the significant aspects of the work's critical edge was not related to the figure of

Sammy Davis, Jr.; rather, it was about what it meant to be a solo performer. Where so many "performance" artists had become skilled at expressing personal anguish and noble adventurousness in cartoonish, comedic, antiheroic, and stylishly *ennui*-laden self-reflection, Horvitz revealed the unrepresentable anguish of otherness. He had a capacity to take what James Baldwin has noted as the cruelty of laughter and place it squarely, sharp side out, between the "you" of the performer and the "me" of the audience. Philip's feat of memory and endurance took him out of himself, to the edge.

When Philip died on the plane, I was coincidentally in San Francisco for a performance. Musician Jon Raskin and I were presenting *Mirror Play* at the Unitarian Church chapel on Geary Street on a double bill with Steve Benson, who performed another brilliant, risky improvisation. Contingency rather than memory held the potent upper hand of this terrible event: the next day, thanks to Kevin Killian, I was able to grieve with Philip's San Francisco friends and to see those of his family, including his father and brothers Lee and Wayne, who had come down from the Sonoma wedding. Many gathered in a loft space near the Mission District and I can almost remember each griever's face, devastated. I also remember the dark grainy floors of the loft and the piano display of photos, including one Philip

had showed me of himself with friends, all exhibit-
ing great goofy fun, at a beach in Mexico. Among
those in the kitchen not touching the big spread on
the nearby table were the artist Scott MacLeod, who
had performed the part of Pelican in *Memory Play*,
and Renny Pritikin and Judy Moran, who directed
80 Langton Street/New Langton Arts in the 1980s
and had been significant supporters of Philip's work.
It is likely I first heard of his work through them.

I spent much of that afternoon seated on a low
stool talking to Philip's brother Lee, a philosopher,
who recounted to me the narrative Philip published
in *Jimmy & Lucy's House of "K"* about his encoun-
ter with Michel Foucault in 1983. He had been an
undergraduate, had had a question about being an
artist, went to Foulcault's office hours, then for a
walk through campus with him. They search for a
café in Central Berkeley. Cafés are scarce, but at last
there is the Rendezvous, where their conversation
holds its own against a radio sex talk show, some-
thing that jazzes Philip since he is talking to the
"king of sexuality." Their conversation moves from
the life of the artist, "The authority is yourself...
there is a difference between playing in the structure
and with it," to AIDS. Foucault appears to be ex-
hausted.[1] "How can I be scared of AIDS when I
could die in a car." They walk to the BART Station.
Foucault, according to Philip's brother, looks up at

Philip as he descends on the BART escalator, and according to Philip's written account, says, "Don't cry for me if I die."

Lee's account dilated time in the manner in which death brings one together with the world, as if there is only connection. I reported to him that the last time I had seen Philip was on New Year's Eve, 2004, when we had read through *Mirror Play* with Annie Kunjappy, the three of us sitting cross-legged on the carpeted floor of his just-acquired tiny apartment on Fifth Avenue and Ninth Street, and had begun to discuss a New York production. Months

---

1. See *Jimmy and Lucy's House Of "K,"* no. 2 (August 1984): 78–80. I was astounded when I realized in the course of conversation with Philip's brother that this was the same issue that had run a number of articles on my work. I did not know Philip at the time and I did not recall his or Johanna Drucker's eulogies to Foucault at the back of the issue, which are followed by "In Memoriam" from Ted on the last page:

> On hearing of Oppen's death I recalled these lines from
> his poem "Daedalus":
>
> > He believed more in the things
> > Than I, and less. Familiar as speech,
> > The family tongue.
>
> —Ted Pearson, 7/84

later I received a note from Lee, who had been sorting out the apartment, about what he should do with things that he thought rightfully belonged to me. One of them was a book by Jean Day, which Philip and I had discussed. He had placed it in a file labeled "Carla."

■

HERE MEMORY OF fellow being becomes a memorial, and a memorial is something installed by and in memory with a community in mind. Whereas, memorization rather than memorializing was a problematic of my plays, dating back to *Percentage*. This is attributable to 1) language being the main event of the performed text, 2) paratactic devices, and 3) the distribution of narrative within nonnarrative and anti-dramatic dialogue. In my performance writing, story when it occurs is narrated by a performer, while in conventional performance the performer is narrated by the story—as if she had never been anywhere else in her life. In my plays, then, even narrative language is hard to memorize because the performer is producing the language of narrative rather than identifying herself as a part of the narrative. If a narrative accommodates the sense that one can enter it as if one has never been any place else, there must be some resonant familiarity, some version one already knows "from the outside." This outside is where everything has already been said then rehearsed many times as if it were true that there are only a few stories to tell, that get told over and over again. The performer enters the groove of the already given and discovers her unique unfolding inside the suffocating legitimacy of the sanctioned story. Conversely, the plays that interest me involve "change in place of calculation."[2] Sometimes it might be better just to make everything up as if one were able to think on one's feet, except that "one" is replaced with a plurality of voices cutting into each other, cutting things up, leaving space for "others," as Ted puts it in his section that follows. The plays present conversation tarnished with spontaneity and lack of goal orientation, dialogue one cannot codify.

> D: True memory is just a glamorous condensa-
> tion. (PERCENTAGE)

D claims true memory is not true. But it is perhaps entertaining or attractive to someone D thinks has been duped. And D might be a bit annoying in her pithy judgments. The audience gets to decide. Whereas, my Grandmother Fox's memory was a spectacle of facts and names sometimes accompa-

---

2. Tom Mandel, "Carla Harryman," in ibid., 24–26.

nied by incidents. A conversation with her was like being inside a very active set of enumerations, as if Deuteronomy had met Gertrude Stein. In *Memory Play* I deliberately attempted to exclude certain kinds of memory often rehearsed in literature, even to great effect, as in Tennessee Williams's *Cat on a Hot Tin Roof*, where traumatic and endlessly rehearsed, yet unprocessed, memory produces the drama of interpersonal dysfunction.

Likewise, Eugene O'Neill's *A Long Day's Journey into Night* subjects its audiences to the tortures of living in memories, of being determined by memories, of not being able to escape memories. Memory in these dramas produces negative life stories, narratives trapped in tragedy and melodrama. Such negative life stories of the American Way, whether they are about self-idealization or horrible shame, are often obsessed with childhood and particularly adolescence—as if the adult were merely an unfortunate vessel for the torment of youth. These works are among those that our culture recognizes and reveres as great representations of its ethos. What they represent is adult management of despair in past fantasies and a corresponding incapacity to change one's psychic life to the degree that everything "outside" *becomes* one's psychic life—stuck in rather than engaged with the past.

A lack of regard for conventional representations of the family romance has everything to do with my critique of American drama. At some point, I saw my somewhat "boyish" nature energetically thrown into a girl's body and mentality and I wanted nothing of arrested development. I wished to keep evolving. But once I recall when I crawled under a table to retrieve an object for a fellow diner at a San Francisco restaurant South of Market—it was Hamburger Mary's around 1978, maybe I was graduating, it was a group that included conceptual artist Jon Winet—my mother, there with my father visiting from Nemole, said, "You always have been a bit boyish." Her remark was witty, if not a little nervous, and kind, devoid entirely of dramatic accusation: "What did I do wrong?" I also recall that I was wearing tight grey pants.

Today and yesterday adult despair is managed by unalloyed work, or the lack thereof. It is therefore unnatural to make a play: Poets Theater is work, but like writing poetry, it is not a job. It makes its way in a nomadic manner, supported by underpaid cultural workers, from fundraisers to the director. A politics of memory, one any number of poets in their engagement with questions of labor have taken up between then and now, speaks to not denying the material conditions under which the work is produced. The material conditions are the work's memory.

Memory can take a beating under the pressure

of economic demands. But a performance writer like Rodrigo Toscano can turn this site of potential tragedy into conditions for "pure experimentation to see what will happen."

The position of the writer is to play with the structure. The antirepresentational aspect of the work is the writer's making apparent a mental not actual world. Simultaneously disclosed and activated is the desire for agency in a present moment. The resulting performativity or play deemphasizes the drama of memory, cancels it out. These are things I might have said in 1970, or '72 or '74 or '78, but I can't remember specifically that I did.

■

PERCENTAGE, AN ACT OF performance writing and a text for performance, was written in the late 70s. It was a demonstration of play, that which deemphasizes drama and turns memory into words freed from stabilized narrative contexts. One might say, drawing from Barrett's critical writings, that it is constructivist, built toward an open horizon. It would have been happy in the temporal interstices of Moscow in the early twentieth century. "Yesterday, some kids found a hidden orchestra pit," and what is anyone going to make of it? A theater in which no money changes hands?

The work has been performed in more circumstances than I can remember, but in the decade of our current discussion, I do recall performances at Theater Artaud and The Farm. Performance artist Jill Scott and Ron Silliman organized the art and literature series at The Farm, making intriguing pairings between conceptual and performance artists and writers. The series attracted substantial audiences. Undoubtedly some small amount of money did change hands.

I remember performing *Percentage* with Eileen Corder in what now feels like cavernous white space. I can't recollect whether or not the floor of the big farm gallery was cement or wood. It was a bare room. We sat in straight-backed chairs facing the audience, speaking without looking at each other as if we were trying to get the words of the text as animated by voices to meet at the apex of an imaginary triangle situated between the two seated performers and the audience. After that, we all went outside to stand in a nicely lit and quite large yard, which might have also been a corral, around which Jill Scott rode a horse.

Jill seemed to be wanting to make a statement, to assert her place in the world. The world then was the art world, in which she was also a horsewoman who had had adventures even beyond my wildest dreams. She had been stranded on a horse ranch in Ethiopia during a period of extreme curfew and later she caught malaria in, I believe, Central Africa, where she was saved by people who wrapped her in leaves and buried her in mud. I remember her telling these stories at breakfast at my parent's house in Nemole on a trip the two of us took there because she wanted to see Disneyland. We went with my mother and my aunt. Jill wanted to see how the Disney illusions worked, so she kept sneaking behind the scenes to look at pulleys and electronic devices.

She emerged from the haunted house delighted by illusions laid bare on the other side of the wall of pop-out ghouls. My family has a history with Disney, as my grandfather was under his employ as a woodworker, so we were able to go there for nothing or close to it. She could get into Disneyland, but it was hard for her to be taken seriously by male artists in San Francisco, a topic of not-infrequent discussion. Jill believed that I was far more fortunate in this respect than she. Perhaps it was this frustration that caused her to package herself in a crate and ship it through the mail to an address I believe was 80 Langton Street. The horse ride seemed to be about

Jill's wanting to produce potent transformation predicated on her invisible past and her current life.

There was a kind of magicianship exercised by some of the San Francisco performance artists of that period, but I never wanted to be a magician.

IN GRADUATE SCHOOL the focus was largely on connections between theory and practice within the framework of conceptual art, performance art, and new and improvised music, but there was one exception. It was a course for women only, something not uncommon in the context of 1970s feminism, as corrective to a history of male-oriented instruction in higher education. In my memory, two themes prevailed: one was a positing of permission and risk-taking against the background of female conditioning that supports passivity and care giving, and the other was self-expression based on documentary evidence of personal history. Although I know that this course and others like it at the time had a beneficial effect on women artists, I would never have taken it had I known what it was about in advance. My work was not autobiographical, would be skeptical about identity based on a presumed common experience, and it was not exactly self-expressive. But I was interested in theories of oppression, a marked-as-masculine and intellectual interest supposedly discontinuous with the politics of personal experience.

Even so, experience proves to be fruitful. For the class I borrowed some Black Sparrow pamphlets of Artaud's work from a boyfriend and wrote several works stealing from Artaud and otherwise rewriting and resisting his text in improvisational tactics that created a derangement between the preexisting work and my composition. I saw myself as assaulting Artaud's misogyny, drawing from its energy but ironically, parodically critiquing his view of the source of the energy and the knowledge that produces misogyny. At the same time "Artaud Denied" was complicit with Artaud against the maneuvers of what at the time I had perceived to be rather simple-minded identity poetics.

> Tortured people come to be recognized by the whole world as the revealed; so although he taught her everything he knew, she didn't care. She permitted him to think whatever he wanted, because his ruthless suspicions, his gorgeous nihilism, which swept the tide of meaning into numbing order, never came near, so she believed, the atrocities, which made up the nebulous world of her thought.
>
> — "Artaud Denied"

The work was later published in *This* 11, but it didn't go over well in class. It was too intellectual, and it didn't tell the truth about my experience. This was in 1977. One evening a woman in the class approached me, informing me that I needed to learn how to use a gun so that I could defend myself against attackers and rapists. She would take me to the shooting range and teach me how to use a weapon, and I could then get a license. I told her that my father had had a good eye and had given up weapons. I meant it, kind of, as a joke. The lore has it he was good with a bow and arrow back in Keyes, Oklahoma, but had decided to give up using it because of his unfair advantage over nature. This would have been some time before or during the Depression. She insisted I needed a gun for protection. I could be killed, and I was living in ignorance of my danger. I insisted it could be the other way round. What if it were me who became a murderer? To her, that would be self-defense, the scenario was quite clear. Even though the scenario is blinded by "the wounded falling in the direction of their wound," I recognize the source of her fear as predicated on intolerance and hatred. To this I could add a personal list of victims I have known.

■

A SCENARIO: October 3, 1978. Barrett's birthday. He was in Spain. It was after work at the American Poetry Archives. I was standing at a streetcar stop in Noe Valley. I can picture the tracks and the corner, the washed-out colors of that intersection. There was a cold, blustery wind, and I was standing next to a man in a black cape, Robert Duncan. I was crossing the street to catch a bus up to his reading at the Grand Piano in the Haight. He wasn't crossing the street but just standing there. I greeted him and told him I was looking forward to his reading. He just looked at me, another one of those peering looks, but different from how I remember Creeley's, not drunken but undecodable. I didn't like it and it wasn't meant to be liked. It affected the way I heard the reading. It was like listening to something that was quite powerful, to somebody else. I am not sure that the reading and the bus stop scene were even on the same day. But I do recall wondering why Duncan wasn't crossing the street. Why was he just standing there with his cape blowing behind him? The whole thing seemed like a vision from out of nowhere.

In this play of memory, I have referred to magicianship, but now I am talking about a self-identified mage. There was almost nothing in my experience, except an encounter with a Freemason in Paris, that I could connect with the mage's hieratic mode in any meaningful way. Even the encounter with the person in Paris, sitting in her apartment drinking tea while she went over some deal about a recording with a musician friend of mine, only impressed me that some people are a bit too involved with a wish to convey they could off you if they wanted to. Those deep mysterious looks are like kitsch filling in a secret. Even so, both encounters were eerie enough for me to write about them.

I find it curious that I was so little affected by the ghosts of the San Francisco Renaissance, or by Beat culture for that matter. They were a backdrop and most of us were variously associated with these histories as an interpretive context for what we were doing: for me the context was slight. This had nothing to do with my regard for the writing of the San Francisco Renaissance or the Beats, or the impact of the circulation of ideas among writers and writings, but rather with identifications I did not form. Of course, it would have been destructive to do so. Significantly for what I am writing here, the dominant poetic cultures that presided over San Francisco positioned themselves compellingly outside the pathology of the American family romance, except that they gave women short shrift. Just so, alterity joins the mainstream—in a big way.

The dilemma of memory, the demand of remembering to fix meaning has always troubled me. This has at times made me feel reluctant to continue with this project: when I was a child I threw away my diaries after I filled them up. In the meantime, I hope I have begun to answer the questions Steve posed in part 1: "How was it the same for you?" "How was it different?" For one thing, all our friends and cohorts weren't known in common or within the same degrees of intimacy and intensity. There are always prospective meetings-up and not only mournful instances of loss, such as that encountered in the company of Philip's brother, in the aftermath of his death. Philip's story of Foucault speaks to this.

■

IF ONE COULD imagine the exteriorized space of our current meeting as neither the surface of a computer nor of a book, how would one describe it?

I'M AMAZED BY the precision of your memories, especially Ron's and Barry's. Mine is vague and full of holes by comparison. I'm trying to remember how the publication of my first book, *Extremities*, came about. For instance, where did the cover art come from? I've just looked at the book but it doesn't say. I think I remember Geoff showing me the image and saying it was done by a friend of his—but I'm not certain. (I also remember Geoff having what seemed like quite a nice house in the East Bay when the rest of us were, for the most part, hanging on by our fingernails.) I don't remember how Geoff came to know my work or choose my book! It seems like I would at least know that. I do remember Tom saying he'd "put a word in." Did that ever happen? At what point in the process? I also remember Barry suggesting—well, it was stronger than a mere suggestion—that these poems could best be experienced in sans serif typeface. I still like the way *Extremities* looks. When Wesleyan republished some of them in *Veil*, they looked strange in their new clothes.

I remember Chuck and I picked up my free copies of the book as we were leaving San Francisco for good. I asked Geoff if I could take fewer copies and have the difference in cash. He acquiesced to what must have seemed like a very strange request. This had something concrete to do with class.

If we are going very deeply into our memories of this period, I'll have to confess that I spent most of the 70s wondering whether I was in or out of the new nexus. (In that way it was a little bit like junior high.) What was this new poetics that later came to be known as "language poetry" and was I part of it or not? My relationship to *This* magazine, for instance, felt a little strained to me. I had poems in *This* 2 in the early 70s when it was still in Iowa. Maybe Ron had suggested I send poems there? At some point I got a letter from Barry suggesting that I send more poems. Apparently, I didn't respond. Maybe my daily life was overwhelming on the day I got the letter. (Chuck and I were in San Diego then, living in a big, old house with a large group of raucous slackers. I wouldn't really call it a commune. I was too introverted to be a good fit in this situation.) And I didn't have a very serious conception of my career as a poet at the time.

Somehow I thought his solicitation of my work must have been generic, a mass mailing. Now I know how ridiculous that sounds. Later, in about '73, I first met Barry when Jim Preston brought him by my house on California Street. Right away he questioned me about not having responded to the letter. I told him I hadn't seen it as personal. (Did I think it was like a sweepstakes mailer? "You may already be a winner.") Of course, he looked at me askance. Eventually I had work in *This* 5. Then, for what seemed like the long stretch between *This* 5 and 10, my work did not appear. Apparently, it didn't exemplify the poetics Barry was developing. Perhaps it was too lyrical. Has anyone anywhere ever defined what they meant by "lyrical"?

And I remember sitting in my living room on Sanchez Street with Ron in the mid 70s while he told me about a special issue of *Alcheringa* he was editing devoted to this new sort of poetry. He wasn't including my work he told me, not because he didn't like it, but because it didn't fit. "Nonreferentiality" seemed, at that point, to be a salient feature of the new style. I even tried to write something nonreferential, but it was a dismal failure. I was pretty doubtful about what I was hearing anyway. I wasn't convinced that language could be nonreferential and, if it could, I wasn't sure I would be interested in the result. As time went by, nonreferentiality seemed to become a nonissue.

I remember I was really impressed with Barry's *Opera—Works* when it came out. I read it over many times. In fact, when he read from it in San Diego a few years ago, I realized that I knew some of those poems almost by heart. And I also remember how it felt to hear Ron read *Ketjak* for the first time. I could hear the form as it began to unfold and I knew I'd never heard anything like that before. It was almost scary. By that time, it was becoming clear to me that I liked this new writing. But did it like me? For a long time I felt marginal, caught in a push/pull of invitation and rebuff.

How did I come to coordinate the Grand Piano series? I think Tom suggested it—and I'm very glad

I said yes. That may have been the first time I voluntarily accepted an ongoing responsibility! And I felt really at home at the Piano like few places before or since.

The last time I felt excluded was when *Change,* a French magazine, devoted an issue to Language writing and didn't include my work. (This is the sort of thing I have no trouble recalling.) It turned out not to matter, I guess, in the long run—but none of us could have known that then. As time went by and the retrospective anthologies came out, I was presented time and again as a Language poet. It has become a sort of fact. People now seem to think of the Language group as a stable, self-evident cohort—but it wasn't always so.

There was a lot of philosophical and political debate then, as I recall, but on the other hand, very little discussion of why we liked the work we liked. Somewhat later people did write "poetics statements" such as Lyn's "The Rejection of Closure" (a brilliant essay). Still, in our group, as in the literary world in general, people were reluctant to talk about aesthetics. I know it's a minefield. We all find certain things "beautiful," but do we want to valorize beauty? If so, whose beauty? Is beauty an asset or a problem? What makes something beautiful anyway? I wonder to what extent we would agree on that. On his blog, Ron often praises poets for the way assonance or some other sonic device organizes their work. I respond to this aspect of poetry too. But what makes it good? Is it important? Why? And that's one of the less troublesome questions. What about irony? Do we like it? How much of it?

To some extent, to be fair, I may have been marginal because I stayed on the margins.

One thing I can say is that I'm not sure where my poetry comes from. Let's say there's an invisible point in space with a peculiar magnetic resonance of

some kind. Let's call that resonance my poetry. I've always been afraid that, if I left that metaphorical spot and ventured too far towards ______, I wouldn't be able to find my way back again.

WRITING IS AN AID TO MEMORY: this is a seemingly straightforward proposition. Make a note to yourself, make a list to help you remember what you need at the grocery store: lettuce, flour, laundry detergent, salmon, spinach, orzo, tea. Your attention, freed of the task of remembering, can cast about for other things as you shop. Two wo-men, a mother and her adult daughter whom she's come to visit, are awkward-ly shopping together in the produce

area. The mother is tentative. The daughter assigns her a task ("Why don't you do the salad?"). The mother reaches hesitantly for a bell pepper, wanting to put together a salad of the sort her daughter is imagining but not knowing what to put into it. She has conceded her authority. Her daughter bears that authority now, and—brisk, slender, competent, slightly officious—she carries on her performance almost too well. I'd forgotten them—the mother in gray slacks and red sweater, the daughter in jeans and wearing a black blazer—until I had begun to write this paragraph.

When I began work in 1977 on the book to which, early on, I gave the title *Writing Is an Aid to Memory*, I had a point, but it had to do not with lists but with the active phenomenological capacity of writing. I wanted to test it as a medium for thinking, that is, for putting things together, in acts of productive invention and heuristic synthesis. Much as I enjoy the "list poems" of, say, Ted Berrigan, Bernadette Mayer, or Jack Collom, *Writing Is an Aid to Memory* bears no relation to one. I don't deny being attracted to sheer data—but sheer data is like a lexicon, and though one wants to know as many words as possible, the essential thing is to put them together. Experience suggested that writing is indeed an aid to memory, but not solely, or even most significantly, because it can serve as a replacement for memory (which is what a list does). The writing I was proposing was not being marshaled as a cure for forgetfulness. It could be argued, as Thamus does in Plato's *Phaedrus,* when the Egyptian god Theuth offers him the gift of writing: "This discovery of yours will create forgetfulness in the learners' souls, because they will not use their memories; they will trust to the external written characters and not remember of themselves. The specific which you have discovered is an aid not to memory, but to reminiscence." My motives in composing *Writing Is an Aid to Memory* were contrary to those of reminiscence; the work is neither anecdotal nor diaristic. I was aiming for something encyclopedic; I was interested in epistemology: in consciousness, in knowledge, in the ways that knowledge is organized and structured.

The work starts with an "apple": apple for A, the beginning of writing; apple for knowledge.

I began *Writing Is an Aid to Memory* not long after moving back to Berkeley from Mendocino County. Our house was (and is) just three doors down from the northwest corner of College Avenue and Russell Street, and in the fall of 1977 there was a small café on that corner. At some point within a few weeks of our move to Berkeley, Barrett and Ron were having coffee in that café and spotted me walking by. They invited me to join them and immediately one of them—I don't remember which—remarked that they had just been wondering if I had read Milton.

I, in turn, wondered if the question constituted some kind of test, in which case there was a right and a wrong answer. Something was at stake, not only with respect to whatever future friendship I might have with them but with respect to my relation to myself. I was poised between the past and the future. I hardly knew either Ron or Barrett. I felt vaguely inadequate to the situation but consciously pleased to be sitting with them in a café. I was certain that knowing them was going to be important. I had read Milton and said so and never learned the significance of the question. But I think now that knowledge has represented for me not a paradise lost but a paradise found. When very ill for a period some ten years ago, I consistently found solace in a strangely spiritual sense of the field of language that came to me—all of language, infinitely extensive and leaving nothing out.

apple is shot nod

Why my epistemological obsession? Why do I privilege consciousness and the language of consciousness?

It may be in part because I equate consciousness (consciousness of consciousness, in a dialectical sense) with the will to life. That's a phrase that appears in Gertrude Stein's "Portraits and Repetition," and she credits it to William James (and capitalizes it: "the Will to Life"). For both Stein and James, the will to life entails believing the reality of what the world presents—seeing that as what "world" means. It's not unlike Deleuze's "trust in the world" or the *amor fati* that George Oppen volunteers in "Of Being Numerous." The will to life is a volunteering for consciousness.

One can't help but think of Proust here, and Proustian echoes come back many times in *Writing Is an Aid to Memory* ("what the bed at the window was once," etc.)—not just recorded but sought. As Tolstoi put it, in a diary entry dated March 1, 1897 (when Stein was studying with James at Harvard): "If the complex life of many people takes place entirely on the level of the *unconscious*, then it's as if this life had never been."

That quote is highly suggestive—if it's not only the complex life but the whole life ("this life") that's at stake, then isn't memory being posited implicitly here, as a fundamental, constituent element of consciousness? For Tolstoi, consciousness is the site at which cultural forces and ethical ideals compete, and though the struggle isn't particularly dialectical, it remains compelling as an expression of will to life. The character of Levin in *Anna Karenina* comes immediately to mind, with his soul-searching, his indecisiveness, his ambivalence, his sensitivity to ambiguity, the touching failure of his idealistic agricultural experiments, the product of a desire for knowledge synonymous with a quest for the good.

Consciousness is a site—an occasion for—restlessness. For a period of my life, I was afraid of the restless forces of the unconscious. My obsession with knowledge, then, may bear some relation to the fear of madness that haunted me during my university years—a fear that I would succumb to the isolating, singularizing effects of insanity, that I would lose common (in the sense of shared and shareable) sense, that I would become incomprehensible. To go mad was to be imprisoned in the dream (or, rather, nightmare) world, the world of the unconscious, the world of the unknown and unknowable. I knew it existed, that it was real, that it had occupants and occupation. To be insane was to know them, but in such a way that the knowledge couldn't be made known to others.

apple is shot nod

The apple is on William Tell's head. I remember picturing it there—a goofy image, but one not lacking in pathos. This is a writing of sensation, and from the outset, knowledge is vulnerable.

The book is built of phrases, some generated out of my imagination, others culled from books as I was unpacking and organizing them onto book-shelves in the house we were slowly moving into. The marginalia sentence from *My Life* (to which *Writing Is an Aid to Memory* is something of a precursor), "If there's nothing out the windows look at books," refers directly to the shift of attention from the natural landscape of rural Mendocino County to the literary landscape of the Bay Area that I was undertaking in 1977. I opened books at random, scanning the left margin for suggestive words or phrases and writing them down on sheets of paper or on index cards, along with phrases of my own that came to mind. There was no conceptual motive for restricting myself to the phrases along the left margin of the pages, but it had the practical benefit of keeping my attention on phrase units rather than on larger semantic units (the ideas being articulated in the books). It's because I was scanning only along the left margin of pages that *Writing Is an Aid to Memory* includes a number of part words, many of them suffixes: "ness," "civious," "glish," "cerns," "duce," "mena," etc., and morphemes like "deed," "chant," and "poses," that are words as well as possible word-ends. Whether words or not, these are memes of a sort—small bits of cultural, as well as linguistic, information. Memes were the building units out of which the work was composed.

One of the part words, "deen," got a lot of

attention on the Poetics Listserv administered by SUNY Buffalo's Electronic Poetry Center. In *The Constructivist Moment*, Barrett gives a full account of the discussion that "deen" generated, but the gist of the matter was that there didn't seem to be an English-language word that it was a likely suffix to; "dudeen" seemed the only candidate, defined (by Jeffrey Jullich, who first raised the "deen" question) as "a short tobacco pipe made out of clay," a reference that seems, as Jullich put it, "out of character with the timber of vocabulary Hejinian uses throughout." Since I was never a member of the Listserv, I only heard about the discussion secondhand and didn't give it much thought. Trying to remember the source of "deen," my best guess is that it completes the title of Husserl's *Ideen* (Ideas), which I was attempting to read around the time I was working on *Writing Is an Aid to Memory*. But browsing through the book now in an attempt to corroborate this, I am unable to find anywhere in it the German title broken at a margin into *I/deen*. It would be deemed a bad break by a copy editor. I was reading around in other phenomenological texts at the time, too; maybe it occurs in one of those.

One of the structuring principles governing *Writing Is an Aid to Memory* is alphabetical, in imitation (or acknowledgement) of that of standard reference books. The text was written on a typewriter,

with its nonproportional spacing—all lines begin-
ning with *a* are placed flush against the left hand
margin, lines beginning with *b* start one space in,
lines beginning with *c* start two spaces in, etc. (The
published version of the book was set in a font with
proportional spacing. Barrett did the typesetting,
and in order to replicate my letter-space architec-
ture, he had to contrive a method that was more
complicated than mere tapping on the space bar. His
solution to the problem resulted in a page layout that
was exact and realized my intentions perfectly.)

The part words, which became nonce words in
effect, are elements of discontinuity—structural dis-
continuities, ruptures, occurring by chance although
not irrationally. Discontinuity occurs just as much as
continuity in experience and in consciousness. And
contiguity (of the sort that collage and montage
foreground, for example) is as productive of meaning
as other logics. In *Writing Is an Aid to Memory* I took
advantage of chance. Indeed, writing is an aid to
chance.

Writing Is an Aid to Memory: the title has an
aphoristic quality; it's suggestive and has a certain
resolve. Other aphoristic propositions emerge here
and there in the text: "every season deserves some
care," "animals have humps of dignity sitting pure,"
"arts are several branches of life," "life is quantity
through a language." These and similar moments

throughout the text occur at points where the syntax of the compositional units brings about something like a resolution. They are rhythmic events as much as semantic ones, however, and as such these resolutions are temporary.

I was very much interested in the musical possibilities of suspense and resolution, not so much for their affective power (though I envied music that) as for their logical power. Schubert's C major "String Quintet," in which he seems repeatedly to delay or postpone closure or to reject it outright, had a big influence on my thinking about the ends of poems and about what I could term the temporal variation of cognitive units within them: "poses of building."

But it was in trying to understand transitions within the very early compositions of what was about to become Rova Saxophone Quartet, that I was learning most about compositional rhythm and its capacity for unloosing logic and generating polysemantic relationships.

doors are called joiners
    there are several but the term is who
  work
commonly this pitch its second name
but you are the most beautiful
and mostly linked
    (WRITING IS AN AID TO MEMORY, section 8)

Rova's music, even at that early stage, was one of proliferating eventfulness, and maximal eventfulness was something I wanted in the poem, too.

The textual landscape of *Writing Is an Aid to Memory* emerges out of a dense syntactic field, but the landscape strikes me nonetheless as markedly porous—full of gaps. It is a sentimental text—sentimental in the original, eighteenth-century sense that we know from writings like Lawrence Sterne's *A Sentimental Journey* or *The Life and Opinions of Tristram Shandy*, where exposition or narrative breaks off at the moments of maximal affect, where what's meant is not said. Of early twentieth-century writers, probably no one manages sentimental writing of this order as well as Viktor Shklovsky, although Langston Hughes's two volumes of highly elliptical, vignette-oriented autobiography (*The Big Sea* and *I Wonder as I Wander*), for example, are brilliant achievements in a similar vein. The progress of these works is jagged; they proceed unevenly, by pathetic leaps—that is, from one experience to another incommensurate with it (the notion of the pathetic leap is not my own, but I don't remember where I originally encountered it).

This is not the place for tracking the degradation and politically motivated misappropriation that the rhetoric of sentimentality, and the irony that it effects, have been subject to. Suffice to say that (at least in my view) that history is intricately linked to the history of the bourgeois family as both a political force in, and a manipulable pawn of, capitalism and empire. It is not, therefore, out of sheer perversity that I am interested in rethinking their possibilities or reclaiming them for cultural work whose purpose is the very opposite of manipulation. Brechtian theater, with its interrupted narrative effects (and affects) is a site of such work. So too, I think, are some Language texts. Certainly it was my hope that ellipses and disjunctures would serve as both affectively and structurally dynamic forces in *Writing Is an Aid to Memory*. Insofar as the disjunctures produce an incongruity between what's expressed and what's understood, or between the literal and the expressed, the work is markedly ironic. As Donna Harraway puts it, "Irony is about contradictions that do not resolve into larger wholes, even dialectically, about the tension of holding incompatible things together because both or all are necessary and true.... It is also a rhetorical strategy and a political method, one I would like to see more honoured within socialist-feminism" ("A Cyborg Manifesto").

Whether one regards them as aporias or sublimities, narrative (as distinct from semantic) gaps are an intrinsic feature of temporal consciousness, and it is with temporality that memory (and music)

deals. They are fraught, too, with an often anguished
sense of mental, as well as temporal, limitations.

> prison moves lower on the same page
> the figures seem to throw the whole
> rather than dry
> so violent who seemed careful
> throwing the standard into such errors
> of discovery
> it is some random maximum
>
> (section 23)

If, as I suggested, something like fear of madness
played a role in my turn to consciousness, so too did
my grandfather's library, a full third of which was
devoted to annals of exploration and traveler's jour-
nals along with books by various natural historians,
mostly from the eighteenth and nineteenth centuries.
It was the accounts of discovery rather than the data
provided in them that interested me: I was no scien-
tist, just an armchair adventurer, class-bound and
gender-bound, but at least venturing forth in imagi-
nation. One of my favorite poems was (and remains)
Coleridge's "This Lime-Tree Bower My Prison," a
masterpiece of memory, as it's catalyzed and cath-
ected by writing. Writing is an aid to living danger-
ously—and, with respect to memory, dialectically.

■

Consciousness and the knowledge it activates (though it's equally true that knowledge activates consciousness) are not, in my experience, instruments of control. It wasn't so much to control fear (or madness) as to have something better to do with my mind than obsessively (and perhaps narcissistically) introspect that I turned to epistemology. Consciousness could serve as a medium for coming-to-know—for discovery and acknowledgement of alterity and exteriority, and for altered understanding. It has turned out to be a medium for dialogic and dialectical processes, a medium for *being there* and knowing that *that is happening.* If there's an element of Jamesian stoicism here, is that a surprise?

Beginning another entry I encounter the familiar somberness as I think back toward 1975–80. I find myself typing the same defensive joke: that I can't meet the quota of this project, I don't *have* ten memories. I've told this joke twice already—to Rae and to Lyn.

My memory feels like a Magic 8-Ball, manufactured by Tyco (a hollow plastic oversized black-and-white 8-ball filled with blue liquid in which an icosahedral white die floats with individual memories scripted in raised letters on each of the twenty triangular faces; when the ball is rotated so the transparent window is on top the die floats up to it with one of the memories pressing its letters up against the see-through plastic).

Scene: 1980s or 90s, some college campus, maybe in Maryland. Francie (my wife, Francie Shaw) and I are walking with Bob Grenier. Maybe it's Delaware, maybe I'm giving a reading. But why is Bob there?

Peering more intently I notice that while the raised letters pressing against the window have driven the dark blue liquid to the sides, nevertheless a thin layer of fluid remains between the letters. It adds a kind of feeling tone to the typography, a materiality of language you might say. But you have to unfocus your gaze. Scene: 1980s or 90s, some college campus. Francie and I are walking with Bob Grenier. We pass by an open stadium. The scoreboard displays a slogan in large letters: "We're Number One!" Spelling out the contraction, Grenier, always the tragicomic pedagogue, translates: this is Delaware's way of saying "We Were Number One!"

Grenier's joke doesn't get us back to 1975–80; a stronger effort is required.

Another pedagogical moment. This one involves Grenier more obliquely. It was around 1978, when Francie and I lived in a warehouse on Clyde Street, across a narrow alley from the brick wall I thought Kerouac stared at in "October in the Railroad Earth," and one small block, over gravel and abandoned track, from a major bathhouse where AIDS was unwittingly being spread.

Grenier and Geoff Young were having dinner with Francie and me. Was Francie pregnant with Max? Were there others there? The raised white letters aren't including their names. Bob was talking. He was telling a ghost story more or less, of a kind I'd heard him tell before, always drawn from real life. This one was about him and his daughter Amy. Some years before this, Amy's drawings as a three-to-five-year-old had graced the first three covers of *This*, when Grenier was co-editing it with Barry, but this stage was past. She would have been between nine and eleven now. Sometimes in his stories, and this was one of them, it felt that he had to stretch to reach the level of campy/genuine scariness he wanted.

Grenier and Amy were walking in Franconia, toward the old graveyard, at dusk, through the woods, Amy hadn't wanted to go on the walk in the first place, she was scared, it was past dusk, it was dark, so they had to use a flashlight, but the battery went dead, and then they heard a noise, rustling behind the pine trees, thrashing almost, in the dark, it might have been something big, there were bears, at this time of year, in New Hampshire

and at this point Francie stood up rapidly, taking her plate in both hands, it was full, she had made dinner, or had I? it was spaghetti maybe, salad, I'm pretty sure

and smashed it down on the table so that it broke and half of it ended up on the floor. Her voice was shaking with emotion, but she wasn't shouting, she was speaking with complete passion: it was disgusting to scare children like that

I could say that I'd never heard a person mean what she said to that degree before but I would have no way of knowing how true that would be. My memory sucks. I sometimes put Amy at the table, though Francie would never have smashed the plate in front of her. My own childhood traumas (father, alcohol) projecting their ghosts from offstage. What was the immediate aftermath? Dinner went on. Did I sweep up? Did Francie stay at the table? At any rate she had made a point that initiated a thorough change in the way I thought. It was as if I was being shown a sense I had never noticed before: that words weren't autonomous; they went out into a world where there were other people.

■

THAT'S EXAGGERATED. Of course I had always known that. My mirror neurons have always been too highly polished for my own good.

Grenier had been as much of a pedagogue as I had been willing to accept. The question of his authority was low key, but it was clear, when Barry introduced him to me in Iowa City that he had real purchase on the contemporary poetry scene. Through him I met Creeley and Zukofsky. In *The Marginalization of Poetry* I've given some details of how he talked to me about *Sentences*. Words moved a lot when we looked at them. When I first met Creeley, in Franconia, New Hampshire, where Grenier was teaching, we opened the then-new Something Else Press edition of *Geography and Plays* "sortes virgiliani" style—at random—to divine an answer to the question of whether Grenier should stay in Franconia. Stein's answer was an unequivocal *no*: the sentence the finger pointed at (can't remember whose) was something like (misquoting) "The north will kill you." Poetic knowledge, theatrical.

Later, in San Francisco, for Francie to have rejected Grenier's verbal theater so emphatically (the bear in the woods) was a real wake-up call.

floating in a blue liquid

We're all writing discursive sentences here, and isn't that odd?

To say the obvious: all of this, these attempts

at presenting our pasts, go against an early *don't* that some of us promulgated: critiques of narrative by Ron and others (Bruce Andrews, Steve McCaffery). That *don't* has reverberated for decades, especially in the reception of Language writing: don't try to construct novelizing, technicolored picture windows, which only open onto ideologically fixed theme parks. I promulgated this *don't* myself in an MLA talk, but I wasn't terrifically enthusiastic about what I was saying. I had more fun quoting Stendhal and Mozart's letters.

In my experience we weren't a gathering of writing that grew ultimately out of the *don't* soil of Pound—although that is one common perspective of those who complain about Language poetry from afar—but in fact were spurring one another to find new forms.

My first talk, I stood near our bed in the loft on Folsom Street across from the Ramrod. "Enthusiasm and Memory" could uncharitably be called something of a glorified book report on Alfred Lord's *Singer of Tales*. More charitably put, I was wanting to elaborate an enthusiasm. I was very excited about Homer having been a series of orally composing bards, mechanics of some sort or blues pianists. Poetic knowledge never the same step twice, repeatable, changeable, and in a sense, never memorizable. I didn't say it like that in the talk.

I remember two reactions. Duncan McNaughton was emphatically unconvinced, beet red, memory has it, saying that that approach was simply WRONG, that Homer was HISTORY. And there are in fact all the narrative mirrorings in *The Iliad*, too elaborate for coincidence. (I think McNaughton's beet-red critique was where I first heard about them: Have you read *Archery in the Dark of the Moon*? he asked. Check it out.) Barry, on the other hand, was enthusiastic, saying something like, it was instruction. It sounded like Instruction. I, on the other hand, felt like Ion, the Homeric rhapsode in Plato's *Ion*, trying to say what I thought I heard.

This sounds like I'm trying to remember a dream.

I feel a bit like a nonbeliever, not wanting to look back.

Some time before we moved to San Francisco, Francie and I drove Louis and Celia Zukofsky back from Franconia, where he had, at Grenier's invitation, read *"A"*–22. The life of poetry. In the car, Louis told of Williams visiting, what a slob he could be. He'd pee right in the corner of the bathroom. I didn't believe it, which was a funny feeling. Again, authority showing itself to be nonauthoritative. Ron plays peek-a-boo with this information in the line from *Ketjak*: "The urinary habits of Dr. Williams." Finding out that I had an M.A. in Classics, Zukofsky recited a bit of *"A"*– 23 (and I'm very sorry to say I don't remember which lines they were) and said he was imitating the sound of classical Greek there, "You can hear the *oin* sounds there." I weighed this quickly, as best I could. There were *oi* and *oin* sounds in classical Greek: *poikilothron' athanat' aphrodita* (Sappho), "deathless Aphrodite on her delicate throne." He must have been doing a chronological run-through of the Western literary languages, somehow. It seemed unbelievably ambitious and a slender conceit, both. I couldn't really credit it as a possibility and simultaneously was thoroughly impressed. Why didn't I ask him what Latin sounded like?

Is my recalcitrance toward the past simply a matter of disliking mortality?

Last year, Francie and I were at the Warren Sonbert retrospective at the Anthology Film Archive in New York, where we saw his last film, *Whiplash.* The final shot in the film showed Warren himself walking out in front of a curtain and taking a brief bow while "Gloria" was pounding in the soundtrack. I heard Francie involuntarily saying "Warren" and sobbing. On the screen, there was Warren, living in the shot, while offscreen, Warren the filmmaker, dying, had given Jeff Scher editing and assembling instructions to use footage of himself to stage his moving stele. Warren was saying, I want to be re-

membered for having done it, and here I was, alive.
But those are my words, not his. Not him.

For the sake of art,
modernist coffee, Paris,
it would be nice
to hold some things separate,
let the anxious animal graze outside forever
on museum grass

while, inside, history's waterfall flows upward,
sharp white walls

keeping the vision of taste safe
from the mouth that wants grapes

perpetually bursting into the old original wine:
Make It New.

The Louvre
is the shtetl of shtetls.

Unless our home
is language, raising us

inside its womb. Reading its shifting glitter
I almost forget I ever learned
to write in half-lit

rooms and blocks and days.
There are lives outside

the correction chambers of this page.
Couldn't it be stronger? Time

to stop and name.

> —from "Chaim Soutine," TEN TO ONE

Lyn's piece makes me wonder what we're naming and what we know, once we've learned what we've learned. Poetic knowledge is nothing if not a group phenomenon, but that doesn't make it any the less problematic. Surprisingly often, poets don't know the same thing. The Talks underlined that for me. So what is it that's being known? Having poetic knowledge means you know what exactly? Isn't there a better way to ask the question?

> As I see it, yes.
> Ask again later.
> Better not tell you now.
> Cannot predict now.

> Concentrate and ask again.
> Don't count on it.
> It is certain.
> It is decidedly so.

Most likely.
My sources say no.
My reply is no.
Outlook not so good.

Outlook good.
Reply hazy, try again.
Signs point to yes.
Very doubtful.

Without a doubt.
Yes—definitely.
Yes.
You may rely on it.

Non-Events

Morning turns inside out. The engine
    is diseased, as it spreads along
    approximate ice. High contrast
geometry of person straightens out from
    meandering road. Desperate focus
never looks back. Progress makes possible
    a paralyzed attendant, set apart
    an end to himself (moral noise).

"Morning turns inside out." The problem of other minds. What is our market share of the author function? The author share of the memory function?

Who are the designated others, the ones we want to be with? And then, who are the others? What is the relation between these two kinds of *other*? "The soul selects its own society..." In a moment of primitive magic, the initiate chooses his totem animal—which stays with him for life. A gold-plated pin offered for sale in today's edition of the Sunday *Times*.

I remember heavy flirting with S— (not whom I ended up being with). We had revelatory sex in Ted Greenwald's loft during the final days of one of my early visits to New York. The title of her first book had been a lure for several poets. And with L—, whom I told I drove a sports car (true), but when she visited San Francisco around 1977 she was not impressed with my three-cylinder, two-cycle Saab, which I had bought for $900—at the time an enormous sum for me. And whose transmission I promptly had to replace for $700.

Where did I get the money? That, in itself, is one of the most unanswerable questions about this period. (A scrutiny of Social Security and tax records decades later discloses little reported income.

How did I manage to make out?)

> Until we advance nothing seems possible
> until a bridge is built upon us.
> Window openings scale the divorced
> speed of rooms to permanent time. What
> foundations a stone supports, rolling hills
> collapse. In this utopia the common
> bond lowers threshold of doubt.
> A virtual x-axis, crowded by on-looking I's.

Mechanics who dealt with me at the time hated to see me coming. I remember a series of love/hate relationships with mechanics. I must have conveyed an affect of raw vulnerability and unfocused aggression to them. An effect of the exposure I had been through—to nothing they could imagine. How to witness and adjust the vulnerability of the young man's broken transmission? Ralph Gutlohn and I made jokes about that transmission, after we had driven the Saab to New York—where I took on potholes and manhole covers in a frontal assault. John Godfrey, a poet Hannah Wiener once called a "wise man," sat in back as I drove, clearly horrified.

L— was, however, impressed by my relation to Bill Berkson, who published my first book. I will never cease to be grateful for that act of intellectual generosity, given that I thought Berkson was the class antagonist at the time. Likely he did not have the same thoughts about me—as he acquiesced to letting me handle typesetting and design arrangements for *Opera—Works*, which, with its ox-blood red cover, certainly turned out unlike any other Big Sky book. What was inside—set entirely in boldface type —was markedly different as well. It was controversial in New York, but Larry Fagin liked "Dream: With Wittgenstein." Robert Creeley said he thought some of the poems in it were good, but a more class-bound San Francisco poet nearly choked when I gave him a copy and suggested it should have been edited. As it later was, but not heavily, in *Frame*.

I remember telling Kit that the cover photograph—of an industrial rooftop with a triangular vent precisely in the apex of two descending slopes —represented a particular way of looking at sex. At the female sex. And that the back cover—a row of endless windows in an industrial building—was meant to convey the inevitability of fate as an endless monologue of seriality (serial monogamy?), the opposite of any decisive event. Such as sex.

It was Ron who suggested a title for the book, from the first line of one of its poems. "That's what you should call it: *Opera—Works*." And I could only agree. Later I told Robert Duncan that the "opera" in the title was partly a reference to him. "Yes," he said, "I like all kinds of opera singing: arias, recitatives, choral passages . . ." I might mention here that the dash in the title of *Opera—Works* meant "not," and that the preferred locus of value was "works." "Yes," I would tell him, "I like all kinds of work: you have pickaxes, cement mixers, forklifts . . ."

> Different landscapes balance matters
> with the force of clear ideas.
> A blueprint for flood channels
> empties music of its sound. Notice a trap
> made for oneself. Out of the constant
> bright wounds circumscribe the work.
> You becomes another constant, unresolved
> war of nerves on a separate planet.

I was lusting for the stability of structure, in which the foreknowledge is absolute. Death and the young man. I would pour my energies into it forthwith. Bill Berkson phrased this perfectly, in his poem "Negative" with its logic of push/pull. For him, the stasis of energy meeting its equal resistance was a technical note to an effect of art, while for me it was a description of a social process by which one is brought into one's fate. The outcome is fixed as the structure from which one emerged but in which one can only act. "You are left wondering if just/holding [the door] wouldn't involve exactly the/same level of force." Hans Hoffmann as pure dialectician.

Philip Guston as class cartoonist.

For "push/pull" one can substitute "form/content" or "poetry/prose" (or any similar figure for attraction and repulsion) and hone in on the dialectic. Only structure survives—I mean, only value endures. Or nothing: because structure returns back on itself, and we disappear, along with our notions of value. "Money doesn't care if you love it."

That all energy and form return to the mode of production out of which they emerge: this was the problem of culture for the newly educated Marxist. However decisive the poem might be, its agonistic excess placed at the crux of a decision that might have fateful consequences—it had been anticipated. "The foreknowledge is absolute." Absorption returns us to structure—never, certainly, to our rewards. The idea of art acquiring symbolic capital—prestige, the surety of the canon—was unthinkable at the time. Art was an addition to a fully rationalized world and thus subject to immediate reintegration. Art could appear or disappear at will, as it did. I thought this insight was progressive, and I intended to act on it.

One of my jobs at the time involved typing address labels for a pornographic film distributor. On the day I received my NEA grant, I was working on the menu for a gay hotdog stand called "Hot and Hunky." I remember being chained to my seat at the West Coast Print Center for days on end, typing populist poetry, porn novels, and vanity memorabilia. It has been noted that I typeset and designed numerous small press poetry books published in San Francisco in the 1970s. I learned from all of them. There was a Public Works mentality in the air, to which many of us consciously referred. We thought the NEA might be another version of the WPA.

A primitive continent in the head
cries out for armor. Weapons
anticipate emptying the world
of general ideas. Counterpoint materials
to a vanishing forest of lines. The sun
disappears behind a curtain.
Each man is isolated by design
flaws in his perception of the opaque.

I remember Julia Newman and Betty Berenson. About as close as I got to the Duncan circle after my arrival in San Francisco was its lesbian wing. The Tenth Muse was the name of Julia's mail-order bookstore on 21st and Wisconsin. I catalogued most of her collection of small press poetry and magazines. Much later, introducing Jean Day at a poetry reading, Geoff Young praised her by saying she knew more about the small press than I did. Which must have meant that, until her moment of succession, I knew a lot. But what did that knowledge *mean*?

I would walk from my cataloguing job on Potrero Hill to my apartment on 22nd and Guerrero. As later, I would walk to my job in the porn business (obtained through one of the aforementioned muses) from 17th and Missouri across China Basin to somewhere below Mission Street. I remember my father visiting me about that time as I set off on one of my walks—as preferred alternative to public transportation. I do not remember quitting that job, but it must have been shortly after I refused to take the "Fuck-a-Rama" test required of all employees. This involved being shut in a closet and shown a film that was a collage of every conceivable porn scenario, on the theory that when one was overloaded with such images, one could not deny what one really wanted. A declaration of sexual preference was important, it seemed, for the daily working relations of the staff.

I hereby apologize for all typographic errors introduced into the magazines and books I worked on in the 1970s. I am sure there were many. I remember R— lamenting in print somewhere the corrupted state of the first edition of Theodore Enslin's *Ranger*—a poem I really disliked. Later, I was happy to learn that André Breton had been fired as a proofreader of Proust. Of course, I never intentionally made any typographic mistake. My errors and wrecks surround me ... error was part of my aesthetics. Preserving error to some degree—as any encounter with the world could be erroneous—seemed an ethical imperative to me. I have not kept copies of any of those books.

I remember finding a copy of Ishmael Reed's anthology of California poetry, *Califia*, which I had worked on in 1976, at a dumpy used bookstore in Royal Oak, Michigan. I told the clerk when I bought it that I had typeset the book. His response to that was a complete blank. Editors and compositors do not have rights to credit in most publications. I have always felt editorial and production work to be an ethical imperative for a writer, a necessity of labor and art. Walt Whitman precedes me in this belief. He may be called the first worker poet, as All-American as the Haymarket Riots.

> The eyes wear glasses on the open boat.
> The rubbish heaps are rhythmically arranged.
> Electrical communication beset with
> cheap nihilism reflects monotony of
> industrial work. Lost illusions return
> as symptoms curving against the grain.
> The tools are vanishing henchmen
> of a dull country built by lies.

Correcting proofs. Of many moments of error and vulnerability—and I experienced many at the time, so intense that I thought they could be literally fatal for anyone who witnessed them. I can think of several people, in fact, who have since died as a result of having witnessed my error and vulnerability (or so I thought). For this reason alone it is essential to overcome such defective aspects of one's personality. This is not a matter, merely, of personal growth and awareness. Whitman, too, was a corrector of the proofs of his own error and vulnerability.

Such dangerous vulnerability is what Leslie Scalapino risked when she titled her first book *The Woman Who Could Read the Mind of Dogs*, or Kit when he titled an unpublished MS "Running Dogs." Terms such as "running dog" or "lackey" had an insinuating connotation from the Leftist press of the period, meaning one who was a mere servant to a structure of power he could do nothing about. But we would do something about it: risk our coherence in order to establish the grounds from which we could speak. The risk of coherence was the imperative to locate the limits one was within—limits of knowledge, reason, the possibility of statement. Berkson's rejoinder to such concerns at the time was decisive: "All bottoms are false." But I was a Marxist, not an ironist, and had to locate the grounds of my belief in a relentlessly methodical way—or one could simply give up and move to New York, where "it's turtles all the way down." (Later readings in pragmatism would help overcome such need for underlying support.)

I was not Martin Eden, but like him had a problem with class. Why not be conscious of it? I remember Creeley saying, "The problem with you guys is … you're intellectuals. Too effete. Why don't you get off it and talk to the people?" And then being invited for dinner at M—'s, whose upscale housemate had just bought a painting that was reproduced in a review of the artist's show in the *Chronicle* the day before. Now it was hanging in his apartment. Art as property: what a novel idea. An idea that novels like *Martin Eden* were written to disprove.

I remember C— being put off by the awkward realism of *Martin Eden*—by the writing of course, rather than the hero's conflicted masculinity, though gender politics was likely more to the point.

> Beyond silent clouds the synthetic music
> breaks into number. The basic skull
> cuts deep into unnatural surface of
> semantic field. Floodlights hit a momentary
> dissolve weight under trees.
> In cities governed by loudspeaker
> hypothetical statues assimilate blur.
> Daily life rises from fear of reprisal.

At Berkeley I wrote a paper that argued that the problem of the class structure of art could be solved by inviting bourgeois society to a mammoth art opening and then destroying the building with them all inside. A modest proposal, which earned a grade of A–; I'm glad it was not taken seriously. Recently, at a concert of the Chamber Music Society of Detroit, I was a member of exactly the same crowd. I would have been buried with concrete slabs and I-beams had my scenario been realized. As Kit wrote, voicing a similar thought: "I destroyed 530 Bush." (But I have just learned he was working on a demolition crew and had authorized entry.)

While Williams toyed with ideas of destruction in *Spring & All*, he later backed off from the Russian Revolution: "We have cut out the cancer but / who knows? perhaps the patient will die." There is a persistent lure to performing such surgery on oneself, to know the results of the experiment. The lure of destruction as self-knowledge. "The patient is anybody, anything / worthless that I desire." I remember reading with fascination about a man who wanted to remain in a permanent psychedelic ecstasy and achieved it by boring a quarter-inch hole in the top of his head. How did he know the procedure would lead to that result? "What we lacked was / everything. It is in the middle of / everything. Not to have." Then there was a cult of water drinkers who maintained themselves in a delirious state by drinking gallons of water at a time. As Boris Yeltsin later said, "It was an unfortunate experiment carried out on our territory."

I was serious. So was Martin Eden. I remember going out with a slightly older woman who told me that her goal in life was to find an artist to have babies with. Her desire was not entirely for art, but it seemed only to a degree misplaced. I thought she was entirely sincere, and the sex was dazzling.

And J—, whom I identified with because she felt she had been unduly criticized by her middle-class mother for what she wanted to do. She wanted to be a job printer, and I believe went on to do just that. There was a compact, expressed in sexual terms, of our meeting at the extremes. The sincerity of sex is finding oneself at the extreme of desire, and locating another there. A compact *in extremis*, no matter if it works out. That is knowledge. I'm not sure her career as a printer worked out: she was later unhappy in a brief marriage to one not of her class, and then a single mother with a child to support.

> Pale submission arises in the climate
> of relative work. Death becomes
> a small building in a blinding wind.
> Every trivial verity dislocates the perfect
> tower of dreams. The private tension
> telescopes horizons into points.
> Hysteria annihilates clear ideas to clash
> of precursors bursting through technique.

J— helped me set up the print run for the first edition of Clark Coolidge's *The Maintains*, published by This in 1974 but printed by Maud Gonne Press, a second-wave feminist collective. She had to argue with her partner that it was politically correct to print a work of art to begin with, and one that was entirely dissociative, not affirming class or gender identity as well. Finally, they went through with it but bound in many sheets of paper they had stepped on with their second-wave feminist boots. Anyone with a copy of *The Maintains* with boot prints on the pages (or heavily smudged pages that her partner had refused to cull) should consider it a priceless memento of its moment of emergence.

I remember Berkson's fascination with the Left writers he encountered in San Francisco. I imagined this to be almost a naturalist's fascination, as if these were species of fauna one would never encounter in New York. I liked to think that H— and I were at opposing ends of the spectrum of such specimens of social nature. H— believed in the destruction of art as a basis for community; in his urban guerrilla aesthetic commune, art was a dirty word and they had multiple sex partners, someone said. Poetry must devolve into prose (he advocated a poetry that was as literal as possible, a kind of rhetoricized reportage on the conditions of everyday life)—and then disappear into life entirely. A negation of the negation, with art as initial deviation toward a transformed or reconstructed life, in which the middle class sheds its reification as it is raised to a higher level of historical necessity by means of a downward movement.

H— has since gone on to write some interesting books, without apology for his earlier intellectual excesses. His was a romantic collectivism, I liked to think (which supports a relationship between collectivism and sex). It also went along with his sense of Jewish alterity, a position unavailable to me. A growing antagonism between art and community was beginning to devolve from a common source in the downward mobility of Left intellectuals (or the cultural assertion of Jewish intellectuals). Expression versus construction. When I wrote the infamous line "Stalin as linguist," I was positing a common point of origin for both language and expression. I still seek a theoretical explanation for the varieties of ideology produced on the Left. Later, a number of us would try to think this issue through in "Aesthetic Tendency and the Politics of Poetry."

Bob Glück and I saw each other as opposites on the coordinates of poetry and prose, politics and art. "You think I'm Breton and you're Bataille," I remember saying to him once directly. But on another occasion I intentionally reversed them, causing some confusion: "You think I'm Bataille and you're Breton." "No, no," he said, "It's the other way around."

By the time Bruce Boone attacked the Language
school in Sartrean terms around 1980 (as posers
whose political will was coopted by the aesthetic),
these positions had all been worked out as mutually
confirming.

> Algebraic murderers sleep in these beds.
> The clock buries the cartographer
> > in the flowering cliff. Shadows
> > of zealots rotate 180 degrees.
> The stiff uniforms of disappointed women
> destroy the satisfaction of their work.
> > The workmen struggle with baggage
> > burning with a blue flame.

It was Berkson who put me in touch with Bill
Rock, legendary typesetter of *Socialist Review* as
well as of numerous small press poetry books. At
least he was a legend to me from the moment I met
him—a man who never slept in order to fulfill his
obligations to the Revolution, to be enacted in the
typesetting and correcting of tens of thousands of
pages of proof. "How many pages of *Socialist Review*
(or *New German Critique*) would it take to stop a bul-
let?" was a question we frequently asked at the time.
Tens of thousands of pages of Leftist writing were
produced in 1970s San Francisco, most of it typeset
by Bill Rock. Talk about the material text!

When he was not setting type, between the hours of 3 and 6 in the morning, he would let me in to his Diamond Heights bungalow to work on his IBM compositor, on which I set several issues of *Big Sky*. Teenagers from the neighborhood projects would also come and go through the night. He was providing a safe house for them; there was always the chance a drug deal might turn sour when I was around. Later, I would bring manuscripts to a house on 30th and Market in Oakland, where the action was even more intense, eventually resulting in his leaving the area. I wonder if he is still setting type. The only time I ever saw Bill when he was not setting type was when I ran into him one summer day on Ocean Beach, bare-chested and exposed to the light. I can still see his long red beard flowing over a muscular, sunburned torso.

I liked Rock because he made no distinction between kinds of liberation. The liberation to be gained through political action was, for him, as valid as that to be obtained through writing and art. There was only the question of real-time commitment, the realization of revolutionary will. It was Rock who provided an example of anti-essentialist critique years before I read Derrida. This was a literary politics in which what was truly important was action, not a second-order construction of value. The labor theory of value subtends everything I do; it is the direct inheritance of Whitman and Zukofsky.

The working class came to these shores and built row upon row of houses. They line up like that: railroad flats and the Victorians of the Mission District and Potrero Hill. We inhabited their rooms with a sense of their original use, as we ripped out wallpaper and sanded down floors. Now they are the pinnacle of real estate, the Cup All Dot-commers Race 4. The coincidence of their history and our social address, in all its contradictions, was an index to the present. We were assured in knowing there were an equal number of positions above us as below. Those looming gas tanks had to come from some-where—as likewise the condominiums of Diamond Heights. The cover of *This* 7: an array of gas tanks in China Basin as an allegory of personal identity. If "my inheritance is my date of birth," its objective correlative was—gas tanks. Rational necessity and aesthetic irony conjoin as a historical index.

> Hunger coalesces in huge time sockets
> lost in imagined future. Instant replay
> of recent war balances weight of air.
> Whatever obscures common speech
> locates barriers under ground. Landscape
> in perspective touches bottom of
> architectural well. Forgotten upheavals
> pulse continually in major key.

My inheritance was my sex: of course, anyone can feel this way at that time of life. As Ted Berrigan wrote, "They have sex in their pockets." Destiny is located in the act, and no one is sure how it will turn out. So we are drawn back, again and again, to a point of disidentification as the source of all one is. Some people want to get it over with as soon as possible; others construct an entire life around prolonging its blissful anguish. Certainly, there is never cause for regret. My date of birth is my "missing X": there is no other inheritance. I wish I could make that transparently clear to everyone I know. (It occurs to me now that D— will know what I mean.)

We consigned ourselves to the history of our choice, in at least two senses: in terms of that which was chosen, and that which was not. There was, for instance, the "other" C—, whom Bob was very taken with. I remember a rendezvous with her in the packed bar of Breen's, below the Museum of Conceptual Art on the night of one its openings. This was when my relations with the other C— were still up in the air. "How is the 'other C—,'" Bob liked to say. Signifier and signified had not yet found a common ground in the affections, it seems.

I wonder if this is what Ron meant by *The Alphabet*—a displaced register of intimate relations, sorted by name, in a kind of address book? What else could he want with all those dedications but to stay connected to his lovers and friends?

Maybe that's what the Language school was really all about—a promiscuous encounter with the other, on the order of a Fuck-a-Rama. I advance this unlikely theory because there are still those for whom *language* is only another name for "repression." For whom to be "humped by yours truly" (after the title of a younger poet's work that came to my attention in the mid 90s) is the height of abstraction, a fundamental denial of the body's plan. That language is nothing more than a moment of alienated othering, the alienation of being as other—undermining all belief in the self. But the turn to language is not merely an act of self-denial; it has a historical dimension the poetasters do not usually comprehend.

> The electro-library of illusory lingo
> describes little-known background info.
> Muscular ABC's correspond to
> schematic interior stage-settings.
> Eye-opening narrative purifies throwbacks
> pining for arcane illumination. Agitated
> scrabble self-destructs its matrix.
> Dream flux breaks down to a priori slogans.

To what extent is that history my own? I freely admit it is shared by others, by many who are *not me*.

Once in New York, L— set me up to help in an affair of her own concern. We spent a relatively uneventful night on a mattress on the floor of her apartment, but she forgot to tell me her *other* man had a key. In the morning there followed a strange encounter in which my only response was to repeat, loudly, my name. Later, I returned some clothing she had lent me—it turned out to be *his*—to her at a book fair in Bryant Park. This story has as much to do with becoming an artist as any other. For such reasons, I have always treasured my visits to New York.

Between sex and work there was writing, or so it seemed at the time. The point of writing this now is that there is an upgrading of oneself that should be discouraged, in terms of what motivated me then. If there is a writing of history, as Charles Olson said, we need to see the roots, where one is coming from. Between X and Y, there was nothing. The point of writing this now is that certain aspects of self—nonself, really—are inadmissible later in art. One needs to stick to one's understanding of that point.

A point that recurs in its protensions and retentions, generalized forward and rescripted backward. What I wanted was a *total syntax*: the use of a total syntax is to make a statement that is a work of art. One's life is predicated on a series of choices: this is the path I have taken, apart from any other. When I gave my father a copy of my book by that name, his comment was, "You must mean, total *sin* tax." I did not publish another book of criticism for eighteen years, but will have done so by the time that remark has found its resting place in history. Total syntax.

> Hard-core iron cracks the perma-frost
> table-land with vertical plumb-line of radio.
> The laboratory sphinx gravitates
> toward magnetic north. A text operates
> computer dreaming on ancient boundary stones.
> A second-hand teletype translates collective
> anatomy lessons. Common sense mistakes
> building codes for symbiotic dwellings.

There are few boundaries, of time and space, in this version of my account. Protensions and retentions, rewriting my life backward and looking forward from the certain knowledge that it would have been. That is the version I intended.

Just so, I remember back, through miles and miles of memory, a sequence of telephone poles— stretching into the horizon on a flat plain in Nevada. It was not Route 66, but the song was playing on the radio. Driving forward, the telephone poles flowing backward in the rear view mirror.

I can remember back to each of them, from which point I can discern the one previous. And then I remember having this thought when I was eight years old, thinking the telephone poles were extending even farther back into the past, to when I was two, to earlier... I have always known myself at isolated moments of recalling this sequence, even as I know myself in writing it now. It is the first time I have written it down, though it is hinted at in a number of my works. It is their inherent structure. I have always known I *would* write it down, and that it would be the truth of knowing myself since the series first began. This is the moment when I commit that knowledge to the page. Let it not be erased; I want to think forward from that point to the next.

I do not remember the day N— visited the apartment Ron and I shared at 17th and Missouri in 1974. There was someone at the door. Who was that, I asked? Oh, some guy who came up from Santa Barbara because he was interested in my work. What do you think of him? I'm not sure. What could such a visitation have meant to either of us at the time?

> Self-convicted criminal registers address
> with introspection bureau. Artificial
> voices change places with specimens
> of error. The priestly function of hysterics
> emerges from dead-duck prime movers. Word
> listens to mistakes without comment.
> One voice overheating with worn edges
> disrupts the usually smooth chain of command.

I remember meeting N— later, at the Colonnades Bar in New York about 1976 in the company of Ted Greenwald and Tom Raworth. We had a heated discussion over the question of originality, and whether his writing could be compared with mine. I argued for their difference; he insisted that there was something in common between us. I had not yet seen much of his work—and would not publish any of it until 1978 in *This* 9. That same year saw the beginning of *L=A=N=G=U=A=G=E* (but not the concept of *language* in poetry, as is now understood). We then walked halfway up Manhattan, talking nonstop all the way until N— descended into a subway somewhere around 34th Street. I do not remember where I was staying on that trip.

A moment of othering, in retrospect, for which I ought to have been more prepared. I often found myself in N—'s presence, talking nonstop. It was his refusal as well, which we both evidently enjoyed. There is a resistance of two languages that refuse to coincide—midway between enjoyment and denial. What is the relation of this moment to the concept of *language*? The moment when the turn to the *other* becomes one of totalizing abstraction, evidently.

In 1978, after a disastrous encounter with a person of the opposite sex, I proposed to Steve that we collaborate on a long poem to be titled "Non-Events." The original nonevent, for me, was that sex; it suggested itself as a model for what I wanted to do in the work. To be released from a decisive encounter with another so as to generate a wider horizon of meaning, perhaps. To be displaced onto another as a form of knowledge, if not to be confirmed by any particular *other*. In that I was thinking and writing of Steve. The writing we produced became a moment of knowledge in its displacement, a gauging of the limits of ourselves in language.

To accomplish my portion of the text, I sampled material from two sources: the opaque manifestoes of the Russian Constructivists and the personal/processual epic of Theodore Enslin, which I have said I disliked. Self met other in a capacious unfolding of obdurate language. We published the poem that resulted (and it is partly reproduced here). I am still interested in reading it, but believe I have explained it enough.

> The price of dying is charged against
> new brilliance of metal fittings.
> Indestructible front of color and line
> is parceled into still photos. Automatic eye
> works machine ethic into fragile nerve endings.
> Distant relations march forward
> to claim kinship with forgotten past.
> The manual is rewritten one word at a time.

"Morning turns inside out." This writing has been an extended elaboration of that line.

■

How does your writing address the problem of other minds? Or is it otherwise for you?

Etude III
Angles of Incidence

"I know what I have given you. I do not know what you have received" (Antonio Porchia). Perhaps such asymmetry always exists between what one knows of what one is doing and what one is subsequently taken to have done—between the history of a work's construction (replete with gaps and false steps) and the responses of others that, at any moment, will be the history of its reception. Thus, how one's writing addresses those others both conjoins those histories and unpredictably inflects how one's writing is received.

Geneva, 1973. Each morning, before wandering the Vieille Ville, I sat in the park on Ile Rousseau making notes toward what would become the project that occupied my next three decades. Now completed, THE TUNE'S IMAGE comprises eighteen books in a single serial work. Then, however, it was barely a notion, albeit an intensely motivated notion. At the time, I had been writing for nine years and had produced such work as I hoped would lead to poetry. Apparently, it was time to walk through the door.

Parsing Barrett's question, I was drawn to the verb "address"—and then given pause by its object, "the problem of other minds." My first thought was: put "the problem" under erasure and proceed to the question of address. But first, I must acknowledge my grounds for this erasure because my sense of "the problem"—as a powerful illusion—shapes how I address other minds. To begin, I don't accept the Cartesian model of consciousness, nor the solipsism that model enables, nor the arguments by analogy that would resolve "the problem."

My brief travels in Switzerland and Italy were a respite in a difficult time. My mother had died the previous winter, leaving much unfinished between us. And I was then on the verge of leaving graduate school, abetted by the bottomless font of negativity who served as my thesis director. Compounding those issues was my relationship with A—, which, in its ongoing deconstruction of gender roles and assumptions, was, for us both, as emotionally confusing, and at times traumatic, as it was undeniably compelling.

In brief, "the problem of other minds" asks us to justify our belief that other people have inner lives. It asks what warrants our beliefs about—and what makes it possible for us to conceive of—mental states other than our own. In response, I offer this sentence from Wittgenstein: "Just try—in a real case—to doubt someone else's fear or pain." It is not a question of our ability to experience what another person experiences, nor of inferring another's experience by analogy with our own. Rather, it is a question, in Oppen's words, of "what we believe to live with."

In Geneva, I was able to map IN NUCE the initial arc of my project. I resolved to edit my early work, take from it whatever I could, and proceed with map in hand. The practice of serial composition had been on my horizon since the late 1960s. But I knew I had to do some mental rewiring in order to navigate its logic. This I presumed I had begun to do in the intervening years. So I headed to Milan, where over several days I shared an innocent flirtation with a dancer from the Bolshoi Ballet. The upshot of that was a brief encounter with her ill-mannered KGB minders. I left the next morning for Venice.

What I "believe to live with" is that mind is embodied and that other minds exist—regardless of the extent to which the inner lives of others may remain unknowable to me and irrespective of whatever claims to knowledge or to intimacy that I may make upon them. Over time, of course, one can come to assume that one's knowledge of others, fallible though it be, has predictive value. And perhaps our experience of intimacy with others is predicated on such assumptions. But what matters to me is that *other* minds exist. My attraction to difference—in how other minds articulate themselves and so foster the potential for knowledge—is what leads me to seek community with those whose differences I would value.

When I returned to San Francisco, I resumed my relationship with A—, quit grad school, tossed my thesis (a Heideggerian reading of Oppen), and started driving a school bus. The pay was low, the owners mobbed up, the management lame, the kids a handful, the alarm at five in the morn-

Despite Descartes' "methodic doubt," we can know that other minds exist because, as social beings whose existence entails our interdependence, our concept of mindedness is socially constructed (in natural language, and among other minds) and, as Wittgenstein convincingly argues, words qua concepts are defined through application in communally practiced language games. Thus, I would counter the epistemic "problem" with an ontological premise: namely that, as Heidegger claims, our being is *with* others, not with *knowing* others. And it is in the context of being with others—to include reading and writing with others, which we do, even when ostensibly alone— that questions of address and reception arise.

able artwork; Bev Dahlen, her nuanced readings of Freud; Keith Shein, his love of the western deserts and modern Spanish poetry. Jack Marshall and I shared raquetball marathons and good discussions about Russian and Persian poetry. And, with Steve Emerson, who taught me much about editing, I shared wide-ranging talks and extensive correspondence about the New American poets and writers, continental literature, and jazz.

To return to Barrett's question, my writing is addressed To Any Reader, the title of the poem by R. L. Stevenson that led me to seek out poetry as a child, but which, as a rubric, is not ingenuous. *To* invokes an addresser and an addressee, each constituted by a message—whose transit effects a nexus of relations and whose terms, invariably specific to it, invite interpretive acts. But such relations and acts are by no means universally effected. While poetry is, in theory, available to anyone, it is demonstrably not for everyone. Yet, for any who choose to engage it, it comprises a remarkable diversity of discursive communities and practices. And it is within one or more such communities, as a member of the set of all possible poems, that any given poem seeks reception. As Jack Spicer rightly asserts: "A poem is never to be judged by itself alone. A poem is never by itself alone." And communities of writers and readers are built in consequence of such assertions.

> My earliest encounters with Language writing were utterly serendipitous. Circa 1972, Keith Shein shared a poem that Rae (whom we didn't know) had submitted to TRANSFER. It was, we agreed, impeccable. A few years later, Leora Barish gave me a "mimeo" manuscript of early poems by Barrett. As it happened, she had been at Iowa when he and Bob were there. (She later wrote DESPERATELY SEEKING SUSAN and BASIC INSTINCTS 2, and she directed VENUS RISING). Soon after, Barrett's name came up again, when both Steve Emerson and Bill Berkson recommended that I read his work. After which, the deluge: THIS, TOTTEL'S, TUUMBA, HILLS, MIAM, The Figures, et al.

Though my writing is addressed "to any reader," that address is tempered by its presumption of competence. That is, when a text becomes available, the task of eliciting its meaning devolves upon those prepared to receive it. Given "the set toward the message" that Jakobson identifies with the poetic function, it is a reader's willingness to *engage* "the message"—by which I mean to learn its language, attend to its form, consider its historical and cultural contexts, and thereby elicit its immanent mean-

ings—that has significant probative value in defin-
ing the readers my work desires and the company my
writing addresses.

> I read with interest Rae's memory of wondering
> if she "was in or out of the new nexus." There
> were and perhaps remain those who wonder
> much the same about me. But at the time,
> beyond my own social awkwardness, I felt quite
> free and (as we came to know each other) wel-
> come to actively participate in that "nexus,"
> delighted to find each and all as absorbed in
> their projects as I was in mine. What mattered
> was that this community existed—on the ground,
> actively, in real time—and not my "status" in it.

One sometimes hears that, in those days, the Lan-
guage poets ran a closed shop—a perception of
exclusionary practices that apparently persists in
some quarters. And I want to take that up. In my
experience, such claims reflect the social or literary
anxieties (if not anomie) of their claimants, who
then project these anxieties onto others who are pre-
sumed to have caused or to have failed to allay them.
But if such projections are all-too-human, they also
are all-too-uncritical. One must consider not only
how and that communities may intentionally be
formed, but also how one's relation to them might

MOE'S BOOKS
2476 TELEGRAPH AVE
BERKELEY, CA 94704

BATCH: 176
A-T-M C-A-R-D P-U-R-C-H-A-S-E
75984344
00003000884

REF: 1765
CD TYPE: ATM CARD
TR TYPE: PURCHASE
DATE: JUL 08, 07 14:58:19

PURCH $12.68

TOTAL $12.68

ACCT: 4142
AP: 065819
NETWK: 570   TRC: 751202
RETRIEVAL: 718921751202
SETTLE: 07/09

CARDMEMBER ACKNOWLEDGES RECEIPT OF GOODS
  AND/OR SERVICES IN THE AMOUNT OF THE
TOTAL SHOWN HEREON AND AGREES TO PERFORM
  THE OBLIGATIONS SET FORTH BY THE
CARDMEMBER'S AGREEMENT WITH THE ISSUER

CUSTOMER COPY

contribute to or distract from their development. As Charlie Parker once noted, "This music's about more than wantin' to." And the emphasis here is "the music," not the personalities of the players. If one "wants" to sit in, one's *work* must make sense in the context of what's being played.

> "But the poem itself," writes Kit, "was suspect." And that was the challenge I faced on entering the ambit of The Grand Piano. I knew before I ever read there that my work would invite "suspicion." But that, so I thought, was as it should be, since I and my work were unknown quantities, especially in regard to the poetics emerging there. MY assumption was that one goes home with the poems that brought one to the dance. And by the fall of 1976, I had drafted five of the six texts slated for the opening movement of my project. Given my evident engagement with Oppen and with Zukofsky's shorter poems, the obvious risk I assumed at the time was dismissal as a "neo-Objectivist."

"The risk of coherence," as Barrett notes, "was the imperative to locate the limits one was within—limits of knowledge, reason, the possibility of statement." It was then, however, and remains my experience that "the risk of coherence" cuts both ways.

Work that bares the signs of a radical poetics incurs (as it certainly did in the 70s) the risk of rejection by those whose poetics either disavow such praxis out of hand or who view it as incoherent. Conversely, work that "fails" to display such signs may in turn be dismissed out of hand by some radical practitioners: too coherent, business-as-usual. But in either case, and vested interests aside, there's always the danger of hasty judgments based on failing to read beyond "the signs."

I feel much affection but no nostalgia for the period of which we're writing. Yet I find that my fidelity to the event it was remains curiously and querulously intact. I choose to believe that whatever "suspicions" my mode of address then provoked, they have since been attenuated by time and context, as perhaps my inclusion here suggests. Time was essential for the "angles of incidence" among and between our works and commitments to emerge and be seen as such. As for context, that's adamantly here and now. Here we reflect on where we've been, and now the question, pointed as ever, remains for us—what comes next?

October Song

IX

I'll sing you this October Song
For there is no song before it
The words and tune are none of my own
For my joys and sorrows bore it

For judges like to lay down laws
And rebels like to break them
And the poor priests like to walk in chains
And God likes to forsake them
—The Incredible String Band

WHAT WERE THE RULES of the game and what would it mean to break them? As a young man, I was driven, relentlessly if not consciously, by such questions.

My college career was marked by a series of violations. Freshman year, caught at 3 A.M. with a girl in my room, I was banned from the dorm and dining hall for two weeks, a late instance of the college's quaint punitive practice of "rustication."

Sophomore year I was suspended with a group of forty-seven students for occupying the office of the head of dining halls in a political adventure organized by campus Leftists, including Barnett "Barny" Rubin, in defense of a dining hall worker who had been fired after throwing a dish of jello in the face of a student manager during a work "speed-up."

Junior year was the Revolution. While students on college campuses across the country turned out to protest the bombing of Cambodia, at Yale we struck in support of Bobby Seale, Ericka Huggins, and nine New Haven area Black Panthers arrested for the murder of suspected FBI informant Alex Rackley. On May Day 1970, some thirty thousand people descended on New Haven and occupied the green between the college and the town. The National Guard dispersed the crowd with tear gas. On a platform in the Old Campus quadrangle, Allen Ginsberg sat crosslegged chanting "Om" as the fleeing crowd of demonstrators streamed past. Classes were suspended for the term.

Senior year the custodial and dining hall workers went out on strike. There were acts of minor sabotage and skirmishes with the campus police.

Wittgenstein had sought to cut the Gordian Knot of philosophy by describing thought in terms of language games. Now the rules of the game were up for grabs. One's success or failure depended on which game one was playing.

The invincible logic of American capitalism had led straight to Vietnam. Everyone became suddenly aware of how behavior patterns had been determined by factors of birth, race and class.

What were the rules of poetry and what would

it mean to break them? Poetry was a way to assert autonomy through a drastic reduction in scale. The scale and pace of world events was terrifying and out of control. The poem stood apart. A community began to form around the poem.

A community of friends, "and the subject, always, poetry," this had been the dream of a friend at college, one year older, the child of missionaries in India. After graduation and 1-Y draft deferral (below minimum weight/height ratio), I drove cab for the summer in Boston and drifted out to San Francisco in the fall. Four years later a new poetry community quite suddenly took shape.

But the poem itself was suspect. We discussed "writing" and experimented with prose. Serial works undid the privileged status of the poem. The aerated prose of Creeley's *Presences* lit the way.

New rules were introduced: the limited vocabulary of my *Dolch Stanzas*, the repetition and doubling of sentences in each successive paragraph in Ron's *Ketjak*, the alphabetic indent queues in Lyn's *Writing Is an Aid to Memory*. These self-limiting strategies were designed to open the work up, to push the limits of the "natural," through predefined sets of semantics (*Dolch*), scope creep (*Ketjak*), or field composition (*Memory*).

But the formalism was deeply grounded in an engagement with history as experience, which led

Ron to characterize the work as "realism" in the subtitle of his anthology *In the American Tree*. My concept for the cover of a book to be titled *Entropica*: red block type on a yellow ground, Mexican movie poster style. Mission Street was my *Second Avenue*, a fantasmagoria of twentieth-century *mercantilismo*.

As during the Breshnev years the Russian metarealists, unbeknownst to us, were provoking huge interest as an alternative to state culture, so the New American Poets and their heirs had shared in the rapid conglomeration of restless interest that defined the 60s.

The 70s was the big comedown.

Resistors, condensers, transformers, contact leads, dashpots, timing devices, insulators, solenoids, resistance grids, governor tension sheave assemblies, bearings, car and counterweight buffers, car and counterweight guide rails, top and bottom limit switches, activating cams, compensating equipment, hoistway door interlocks, top trucks, hanger rollers, operating linkages, leveling and encoding systems, lobby fixtures, emergency lighting, communication devices, remote operating and signal equipment. *Bing*: "Going down." It was the beginning of the end of the industrial age.

The Vietnam War bequeathed to Silicon Valley a boatload of radical characteristics: the sense of continuous emergency, the sense of no higher authority, the dependence on improvisation, the endless hours of engagement, the exhaustion and fatigue, the intensely combative mentality, the sacrifice, the *camaraderie.*

Between the twin fevers of 60s radicalism and 80s Reaganism, the 70s was a catastrophic time of heightened contradictions permitting of no satisfactory release. Weird shit happened. The SLA, Dan White, Jim Jones, the Zodiac killer. Days of blurred, static boundaries, recession, gas crisis, hostage crisis. *Aporia, anomie.*

Against the static undertow of dreamy San Francisco, we gathered, as others had and would, *to make something happen.* A questioning, even contentious environment helped focus attention, provoke writing activity. Talks, for instance, where before there had been none outside the universities.

If people were manufactured by the machine called language, then it was time to climb in and reconfigure the machine from the inside.

Aporia: an insoluble contradiction or paradox in a text's meanings. From the Greek *aporos*, "difficulty of passing, impassable."

Anomie: social instability caused by erosion of standards and values. Alienation and purposelessness experienced by a person or a class as a result of lack of standards, values or ideals.

Camaraderie: the spirit of friendly good-fellow-ship.

In an environment of shifting standards and contradiction, a sense of *esprit de corps* became critical. Groups formed along lines of identity politics, back-to-the-land and labor politics, feminism, gay liberation, drugs, music, dance, poetry, what have you.

I had the sense that the stranglehold of ideas, whether those of an inflamed self-consciousness or the command-and-control architecture of ideology itself, could be broken, even by the elements of its own composition, that is, by means of language: "seeing not / dim by dint of / what's not seen" (*Dolch*), so that one could actually see what was right in front of one's face.

"What's going on?" asked Marvin, and his question echoed on the streets and across the loading docks. The answer—"You got it!"—asserted the existence of a kind of balance, a steady state in which the constituents, "everyday people," recognized themselves to be suspended.

On the flip side of stasis lay virtuosity, as in *a.k.a.*, as in *Songs in the Key of Life*, Bob and Stevie pulling out all the stops. Playing every instrument.

One nation under a groove. Steady-state poetics dictated an all-over approach. Later, in *Progress*, Barry wrote the consummate all-over poem, laying everything all out at once, like Pollock, presenting the deep structures entirely out on the surface, in instantaneous recognition of the eternal narrative, retracing the formal progression from *Guardians of the Secret* to *Blue Poles*.

Stories in fractal, adventures of the name. Ripped off its hinges, the story line floats above the bay. Thrum of low pressure, personal history on caster blocks. The seam opens to expose the cartoon. Breathing exercises level off into realms of Brodey.

What caused fissures in the lives of speaking peoples? "That's just an ordinary pain in your heart." Was love a game? Or something moving under the surface, a blindspot moving with the sun, in geological time? Smithson built a low mound of words. Coolidge dented it.

The advantages of a low-pressure economic environment: low cost of living, available marginal employment, free play of alternative organizing principles. We spoke of "the work," but counted on the play of language, its looseness in relation to the variously signified, the uproarious hilarity of its manifold effects.

We experimented with prose and consumed many city blocks on foot. Like the Russian supremacists, we majored in rhythm and tempo, and upon gradua-tion we reported to work at Perididdle Industries.

 IN 1975, WHAT MAY have been the first proto-anthology of what would come to be known as language poetry appeared in *Alcheringa*, a feature that I had edited some two years earlier entitled "The Dwelling Place: 9 Poets." It included work by Bruce Andrews, Barbara Baracks, Clark Coolidge, Lee DeJasu, Ray DiPalma, Robert Grenier, David Melnick, Barrett Watten, and me. *Alcheringa* editor Jerry Rothenberg and I were already talking about the project that would emerge eleven years later as the anthology *In the American Tree*. But even in the 1973 miniature introduction to the *Alcheringa* selection, you can see my anxiety about the concept of groupness & naming:

> 9 poets of the present, average age 28, whose work might be said to "cluster" about such magazines as THIS, BIG DEAL, TOTTEL'S, the recent DOONES supplements, the Andrews-edited issue of TOOTHPICK, etc. Called variously "language centered," "minimal," "non-referential formalism," "diminished referentiality," "structuralist." Not a GROUP but a TENDENCY in the work of many.

Of the nine, only Melnick, Watten, and I were firmly identified with the San Francisco Bay Area.

Baracks had gone to school in Berkeley, but moved back to her native New York in 1973 & by 1975 was moving on in both her aesthetic and personal commitments. Grenier had spent the early seventies teaching at Tufts & Franconia, tho by 1975 he'd returned to the Bay Area & was then living in Bolinas. The office of the prison movement group I was working with in San Rafael was around the corner from the Marin County unemployment office & I could count on Bob to drop by after he had checked in there—we would go across the street to Diller's Deli, purveyor of the best cheesecake I've ever eaten, and have wonderful, rambling discussions, half theory, half gossip.

Another anthology that came out early in 1976 was Michael Lally's *None of the Above: 31 American Poets*. Of the four poets—myself, Andrews, Baracks, & DiPalma—who found themselves in both the *Alcheringa* and Lally anthologies, I was the lone one then living in San Francisco. It's not that Lally didn't include other young poets from the Bay Area—Darrell Gray, Jim Gustafson, George Mattingly, Joanne Kyger, & Hilton Obenzinger are all there—nor that Lally wasn't aware of this emerging tendency among poets (he also included Lynne Dreyer, P. Inman, & Bernadette Mayer), it was that at the midpoint of the 1970s no one not directly connected with Language poetry made any assumptions about

the role of this writing *in San Francisco*, nor the role
of San Francisco for this poetics. In many ways, that
is what the experience captured under the rubric of
Lexi's coffee house seems to me to be about. The peo-
ple involved in that reading series, and in this proj-
ect, transformed each other's lives. To the degree
that we're associated with a literary movement—I
still prefer the concept "moment"—what transpired
during those years profoundly changed both our own
and other people's perceptions as to what a "lan-
guage-centered" writing would be.

To the degree that, when *In the American Tree*
finally appeared in 1986, not only did it have a title
that arose specifically out of Kit's poem and our col-
lective experience in the Bay Area (*In the American
Tree* was also the name of the radio program that
Kit, Lyn, and others had on KPFA), but I felt that
it was utterly necessary to organize the volume into
two broadly geographical halves. Of the poets in the
section entitled *West*, only two were not then living
in the Bay Area—Rae Armantrout, who had spent
many years in San Francisco, & Michael Davidson,
who had grown up in Oakland, graduated from the
same high school as Barrett, & attended San
Francisco State. Even reading that collection today,
what I see is a more loosely federated sense of colle-
giality among the poets of the *East* section, but
something that feels deeply & intuitively cohesive

from those of us in the *West*. The two halves could almost be different books.

For me, this transition was sometimes a difficult, even schizzy, experience. In 1975, I had been publishing for a decade. I'd had three books already, with publishers in Ithaca, New York, Bowling Green, Ohio, & Providence, Rhode Island. In addition to the poem that had appeared in *Alcheringa*, I had work in five other journals that year: *Big Deal*, from New York; *Clown War* from Brooklyn; *Telephone*, again from New York; *Eureka Review* from Willows, California; and *This*, edited by Barrett, my lone San Francisco appearance.

1976 saw a slight shift. I appeared that year in seven different magazines, only two of which—*This* and my own *Tottel's*—were located in the Bay Area. Of the others—*A Hundred Posters, Bezoar, Bondage & Discipline, Flora Danica, & Oculist Witnesses*—the first & last could be said to be integral to this emerging tendency, but if there was any allegiance between the other three beyond some vague "post–New American Poetry" or eclectic mode, I don't recall it.

Even as late as 1979 & '80, I managed to go two years without a single poem in a journal from the Bay Area. What this meant in practice was that I found myself in two very different poetry worlds, one in which I published but communicated largely through the mails, sometimes with people I'd never met, and another characterized by readings (and from 1977 onward, by talks) and face-to-face interactions. The feeling tone of the two worlds was always enormously different and my emotional commitment was always to the latter first. It was frustrating to me at times that I could publish in a journal like Paul Kahn's *Bezoar* only to discover that absolutely nobody else in the Bay Area would see it. And it was frustrating to discover that people outside of the Bay Area seemed to have no clue about this wonderful circumstance I and many other poets were now experiencing.

In the Bay Area, tho, you could tell. You could tell by the audiences at the Grand Piano that had shot up dramatically beyond what poets were used to seeing, say, at the City's one longstanding reading series at Intersection, then in North Beach. Because both reading series originally had been scheduled on the same night of the week, Intersection changed its schedule. And you could tell by the quality of discourse later that evening at the Ab Zum Zum Room, the closest tavern to the Piano. People could go to a reading and come away excited by ideas. We coaxed, challenged, prodded one another, by example as much as anything else, but also by talking, not just at the talks, but all the time. In 1974–75, I lived with Barrett on Missouri Street on Potrero Hill, and then again, in 1977, I moved in with Tom Mandel after my collective household had been scattered in the wake of a rent strike & eviction. And from 1978 to 1980, I lived upstairs from Alan Bernheimer & Melissa Riley, in a flat whose previous tenants had been Kit Robinson & his family.

And, for awhile at least, people who shared very little in the way of our aesthetic preferences were part of the audience at the Piano also, what I used to think of as the "curiosity factor." One consequence of this, tho, was that people who didn't share in these ideas—or who maybe didn't think of ideas as something you shared—would complain. Not all of it was the simplistic anti-intellectualism with which we had to deal with from certain post–New American Poetry types. One conceptual artist explained this to me a few years later as an expression of her scene's frustration that, regardless of what they did, conceptual artists didn't have enough terms in common with each other to be able to build on what one another were doing. Whatever other issues may have been at play among us, an inability to respond to and build on what one another was doing was never one of them.

About THE GRAND PIANO

THE GRAND PIANO is an ongoing experiment in collective autobiography by ten writers originally identified with Language poetry in San Francisco. It takes its name from a coffeehouse at 1607 Haight Street, where between 1976 and 1979 the authors variously organized and took part in a reading and performance series that became a venue for many in the literary community to present and hear new work.

One of the principle goals of *The Grand Piano* has been to recall and contextualize events from the period of the late 1970s, but the issues engaged are by no means confined to those events or to that time frame. A chronology of Grand Piano readings located at the end of part 1 provides a historical record of the series itself. Other documentary materials will be added to volumes as they are published, so that a more complete record of literary events and publications in the period may result.

By the time *The Grand Piano* was begun in 1999, a number of the authors had left the San Francisco Bay Area for locations elsewhere. The project was thus undertaken as an online collaboration, first via an interactive web site and later through a listserv. As originally planned, each author was to follow the prompt of the previous, but as the work has grown in complexity many sections have been written out of order. In the end, there is no simple temporal sequence in the writing, nor do the authors adhere to any prescribed themes. *The Grand Piano*'s development is thus nonlinear, even as it is being published in serial form.

When it is completed, *The Grand Piano* will number ten parts. In each separate volume, the ten authors will appear in a different sequence. The matrix of the projected work is given below. New volumes of *The Grand Piano* are scheduled to appear at three-month intervals until the series of ten volumes is complete.

1	BP	BW	SB	CH	TM	RS	KR	LH	RA	TP
2	BW	TP	RA	SB	KR	TM	RS	CH	LH	BP
3	SB	TM	CH	RA	LH	BP	BW	TP	KR	RS
4	CH	KR	TM	BW	RA	TP	LH	BP	RS	SB
5	TM	RS	BW	TP	SB	RA	BP	KR	CH	LH
6	RS	SB	BP	KR	BW	LH	CH	RA	TP	TM
7	KR	CH	LH	RS	BP	BW	TP	TM	SB	RA
8	LH	RA	RS	BP	TP	KR	TM	SB	BW	CH
9	RA	LH	TP	TM	RS	CH	SB	BW	BP	KR
10	TP	BP	KR	LH	CH	SB	RA	RS	TM	BW

THE GRAND PIANO part 3 is published in an edition
of 1000 copies for Mode A / This Press in April 2007.
Printed by McNaughton & Gunn, Inc., Saline, MI 48176.

PUBLICATION HISTORY: part 1 (ISBN 978-0-9790198-0-7),
November 2006, 80 pp.; part 2 (ISBN 978-9790198-1-
4), January 2007, 96 pp.; part 3 (ISBN 978-9790198-2-
1), April 2007, 128 pp.

ACKNOWLEDGEMENT: a version of "October Song" by Kit
Robinson appeared in 26: A JOURNAL OF POETRY AND POET-
ICS, issue e (2006).

ERRATA: the ISBN for part 1 is incorrectly given on the
jacket, cover, and verso; the correct number is 978-0-
9790198-0-7; part 1, p. 12, lines 3–4, read "to an over-
flowing audience"; p. 77, add "OCTOBER 31: Stephen
Emerson and Ted Pearson" to the Grand Piano read-
ings in 1978; part 2, p. 19, line 3, read "who would be-
come"; p. 25, line 4, read "not long after"; back jacket
flap, read "GARDENER OF STARS (Atelos, 2001)".

ISBN 978-0-9790198-2-1 / $12.95